Applied Linguistics at the Interface

Applied Linguistics at the Interface

Selected papers from the
Annual Meeting of the British Association for Applied Linguistics
University of Leeds, September 2003

Edited by
Mike Baynham,
Alice Deignan and
Goodith White

Advisory Board: Lynne Cameron, Tony Hartley, Sally Johnson, Marilyn Martin Jones, Celia Roberts.

BRITISH ASSOCIATION FOR APPLIED LINGUISTICS
in association with

LONDON   OAKVILLE

Published by

Equinox Publishing Ltd.
UK: Unit 6, The Village, 101 Amies Street, London, SW11 2JW
USA: DBBC, 28 Main Street, Oakville, CT 06779
www.equinoxpub.com

First published 2004

British Library Cataloguing-in-Publication Data
A catalogue record for this book is available from the British Library.

ISBN 1 90476857 1 (paperback)

Library of Congress Cataloging-in-Publication Data
British Association for Applied Linguistics. Meeting (36th : 2003 :
University of Leeds)
Applied linguistics at the interface / Edited by Mike Baynham, Alice
Deignan and Goodith White.
p. cm. -- (British studies in applied linguistics ; v. 19)
Papers selected from the meeting of the British Association for
Applied Linguistics, held Sept. 5, 2003 at the University of Leeds.
Includes bibliographical references.
ISBN 1-904768-57-1 (pb)
1. Applied linguistics--Congresses. I. Baynham, Mike, 1950- II.
Deignan, Alice. III. White, Goodith. IV. Title. V. Series.
P129.B75 2003a
418--dc22   2004015219

Typeset by Catchline, Milton Keynes (www.catchline.com)
Printed and bound in Great Britain by Antony Rowe Ltd.,
Chippenham, Wiltshire

Contents

1 Applied linguistics at the interface: introduction

Mike Baynham, Alice Deignan, Goodith White

University of Leeds

The theme of the BAAL 2003 conference celebrated the productive interface between applied linguistics research and other disciplinary ways of knowing, forms of professional practice and issues of public concern. In choosing this theme we wished to emphasize the interactive nature of applied linguistics research: interacting with other disciplines in the social and human sciences and beyond, interacting with the issues and concerns of professional communities of practice and interacting with current public issues of concern. We wished also to emphasize celebration, because we feel that applied linguistics now has considerable achievements on record in advancing research agenda in these areas. We are not currently talking about programmatic claims, but of sustained programmes of research in such areas as language teaching, medical interaction, translation studies, media discourse, gender studies and many more.

The interaction between applied linguistics and the concerns of professional communities of practice has been effectively addressed in the introduction to the publication arising from BAAL 2002 (Sarangi & van Leeuwen, 2003: 1). We will therefore, in this introduction, particularly focus on the first interaction mentioned above, with other disciplinary ways of knowing. This necessarily evokes the vexed topic of interdisciplinarity, which is, it is perhaps fair to say, more often espoused in research than well understood. A recent paper on the website of the Subject Centre for languages, linguistics and area studies (Ellis, 2003) casts some light, providing a useful overview, both of the development of the concept of interdisciplinarity in the human sciences and the variety of potential interactions between disciplines. Ellis identifies a number of different types of inter-disciplinary study all of which are evidenced in current applied linguistics research:

1. Developing conceptual links using a perspective in one discipline to modify a perspective in another discipline.

2. Recognizing a new level of organisation with its own processes in order to solve unsolved problems within existing disciplines or problems that lie beyond the scope of any one discipline.

3. Using research techniques developed in one discipline to elaborate a theoretical model in another.

4. Modifying and extending a theoretical framework from one domain to apply in another.

5. Developing a new theoretical framework that may reconceptualize research in separate domains as it attempts to integrate them.

6. Addressing broad issues and/or complex questions spanning more than one disciplinary field.

Sarangi and van Leeuwen (2003), in the tradition of Mary Douglas, evoke a rhetoric of purity and danger, contrasting the traditional 'pure' disciplinary framing of Linguistics with the dangerous but productive transgressions of applied linguists, crossing disciplinary boundaries in search of methodologies and theoretical insights that will illuminate the issues they address. From such a perspective, Applied Linguistics is the interdisciplinary discipline par excellence, continually and contingently on the look out for productive theoretical partnerships to investigate real world issues and themes. Some of these interdisciplinarities, as Ellis suggests, are already deeply embedded in our institutional practices, for example in the hyphenated socio- and psycho- linguistics, where decades of work have articulated theory from Sociology and Psychology with linguistics. Others are more emergent, for example in the interaction with cultural studies. The so called 'discursive turn' in the social sciences opens up windows for more productive theme based collaborations across the whole gamut of social sciences research. Although, as we suggested earlier, much has been achieved, much also remains to be done in creating theoretical interfaces and building interdisciplinary links.

With one aspect of Pit Corder's original formulation of applied linguistics, quoted in Sarangi and van Leeuwen (2003: 3) we would profoundly disagree. For Pit Corder 'the applied linguist is a consumer, or user, not a producer, of theories' (Pit Corder, 1973: 10). In our view, the applied linguist today is a producer as much as a consumer of theories, subverting the tired binary distinction between theoretical and applied linguistic knowledge which exercises so many unproductive debates between 'linguists' and 'applied linguists', a discussion of which can be found in Badger's paper in this collection.

Academic literacies has become a significant focus for applied linguistics research over the last decade, a field of research shaped by monographs such as Ivanic (1998), Prior (1998) and Lillis (2001), influential edited collections such as Jones, Turner and Street (1999), Lea and Stierer (2000), key papers such as Bartholomae's seminal 1985 paper 'Inventing the university', as well as numerous journal articles. This strand of applied linguistics research is evidenced in the first three papers of this volume. The research topic is one which lends itself to interdisciplinary perspectives in a number of ways, both theoretical and practical, as we shall see.

Harwood's paper explicitly invokes different disciplinary perspectives on citation analysis, providing what one might call, *pace* Fairclough, an example of 'manifest interdisciplinarity'. The study reported corresponds to Ellis's third type of interdisciplinarity: using research techniques developed in one discipline to elaborate a theoretical model in another. Harwood identifies three fields where citations have been researched: information science, sociology of science and applied linguistics, going on to make use of the information science and sociology of science emphases on citation analysis to critique what he perceives as a somewhat mechanistic tendency in the EAP literature, concerned with the nuts and bolts of the grammar of citation at the expense of its social significance within specific disciplinary communities. In doing so, Harwood's paper intersects with work reported for example in Lea and Stierer (2000) which emphasizes academic writing as social practice. The emphasis on citation analysis is a timely one, as debates continue as to the role of quantitative measures in future UK research assessment exercises. Citation analysis is a very central process in research ranking in the sciences. If it becomes the measure of preference for judging research activity across the board, it will then become a matter of very practical interest for the applied linguistics research community and indeed other arts and social science disciplinary communities. What do we think of citation analysis as a measure of research productivity? Are current citation databases likely to capture the breadth of applied linguistics research? Surely there is a debate to be had here.

Badger's paper seems at first glance resolutely intra-disciplinary, concerned with the debates and arguments we have with each other, the role of journal publishers and editors in fostering the agonistic quality of debate, using the resources of corpus linguistics to track such debates through journal exchanges, some pre-planned or staged and some impromptu. He draws on Lakoff and Johnson's metaphor of argument as war. The pervasiveness of this metaphor is, indeed, interestingly evidenced in Harwood's paper where, in the discussion of social constructivist perspectives on citation analysis, he makes use of expressions such as 'big hitters', 'displaying allegiance to a particular ideological camp', 'payback'. A citation is 'pressganged into service' by writers. These terms foreground military/sporting competition metaphors, suggesting that the social constructivist perspective on citation analysis as a rhetorical activity of constructing powerful speaking positions, cf. Latour's concept of black boxing (Latour, 1987), is a persuasive account of the functions of citation in discourse and the social life of academic communities.

Badger's analysis brings us back to our own Applied Linguistics discourse community, tracking the ideational and interpersonal constructions of three argument sequences taken from the journals *Applied Linguistics*, *ELTJ* and *Lingua*. Sheen engages with Lightbown, Bruton with Skehan, Borsley and Ingham with Stubbs and other applied linguists more broadly. Perhaps this is not interdisciplinarity in action as such, more the marking of boundaries between disciplines and sub-disciplines: as Badger concludes by remarking, 'many of the disputes examined here relate more to questions of boundaries between disciplines than to particular developments...' Collaboration is thus not the only mode of interaction between disciplines. The Borsley and Ingham and Stubbs exchange certainly evokes the interface between Applied Linguistics and Linguistics, reminding us that, behind the fairly benign notion of interfacing implied in our title, is a lively tussle for terrain, that knowledge claims are also claims for space and resources, a place on the disciplinary map, which can be central, peripheral or indeed off the map altogether. Can we understand these agonistic exchanges as themselves a form of interdisciplinarity? Borsley and Ingham certainly intend to challenge the relationship between Linguistics and Applied Linguistics, perhaps exemplifying Ellis's first type of interdisciplinarity: developing conceptual links using a perspective in one discipline to modify a perspective in another. Just as Harwood's paper potentially brings us back to ourselves, reflexively engaging with the ways that knowledge claims are made and held, Badger's paper reminds of the centrality of argument in knowledge construction. The question that hangs in the air in Badger's paper is whether there is another way, whether argument is indeed agonistically wired into knowledge construction, or whether there are other more collaborative ways of engaging in knowledge construction.

Scott and Turner's paper, with its emphasis on disciplinary difference in academic writing practices and the discursive construction of knowledge more generally, challenges the notion of a one size fits all approach to academic discourse. While Harwood and Badger start from the text, Scott and Turner's approach is grounded in practice, in the textual engagements of academic writing tutors and students with heteroglossic text spaces, orchestrations of disciplinary and personal voices, which students struggle to shape into their own texts in myriad writing assignments. Here we find ourselves at another kind of interface between disciplines: the need for academic writing practitioners to engage with the texts and practices of a whole range of disciplines in order to support student clients in writing workshops, writing centers, individual consultations and the like. Interdisciplinarity is in many contexts part of the standard 'rules of engagement' for students in the new university. Students for example on professionally oriented courses such as nursing may be writing as clinicians, as sociologists, as reflective practitioners as philosophers. Academic writing practitioners accompany them through these bewildering heterglossic spaces, helping them, in Bartholomae's memorable phrase, to invent the university as they go. This paper is perhaps closer to the issues of autonomy and communiality of applied linguistics and communities of practice, raised by Sarangi and van Leeuwen (2003).

The second group of papers is concerned with the language learning, and it is interesting, in terms of the recent history of applied linguistics in the UK where a broadening of the scope of applied linguistics away from a primary focus on language teaching may have left some thinking that this original focus had been lost, that papers with a focus on language teaching are in fact the largest group of papers in this volume; at the conference itself it was a significant theme. However, within the theme, the range of contexts studied is wide, reflecting a broadening of interest beyond what might be considered the traditional ground of studies in language learning, that is, post-16 learners of English as a foreign language, often in a private school or university context. In the studies here, the target languages that learners are tackling include English, but also French, German, Spanish and Italian. In terms of context, learners are studying in universities, but also in an elementary school and a secondary school. Each of the five papers concerns itself primarily with factors underlying successful and less successful language learning; nonetheless, the relevance of each study for teaching, and some possible implications, are immediately clear.

In the spirit of the interdisciplinarity of the conference theme, several of the papers in this group adopt theoretical models that have been developed in related fields as a tool in addressing their own concerns. This includes borrowing across sub-disciplines. From the field of L1 acquisition studies, Su and Huang take the Developmental Hierarchy Hypothesis (Goswami & Bryant, 1990). This claims that for children learning English as their mother tongue, phonological awareness develops in a set order, initially at the syllabic level. The researchers use the hypothesis as a framework for the investigation of the development of phonological awareness in Chinese-speaking children learning English.

Kobayashi and Rinnert also take L1 learning into account in their research, which considers the effects of expertise in L1 and L2 on L2 writing processes. Ife's paper shows how computer-held corpora, traditionally used for language description work, can be used to investigate questions about early language acquisition. Reaching further outwards from language learning research, in an interdisciplinary way, Williams draws from research in educational psychology in her development of a model of motivation in language learning, following criticism of established models for over-emphasising social factors. This is an example of Ellis's fourth type of interdisciplinarity: the modification and extension of a theoretical framework from one domain to apply in another.

Methodologically, these five papers show a variety of approaches, each of which combines creativity and rigour. Both Benati and Romero-López, and Su and Huangs' papers also develop methodology to study very detailed aspects of their field. Benati and Romero-López investigate the components of the processing instruction model of grammar teaching, and attempt to determine which produces the clearest effects. They take a number of groups of learners and subject them to differing methods of instruction in order to compare the effects of each on their performance in interpretation tasks and written tasks. The study is strengthened by their innovative decision to use learners of both Italian and Spanish, and to compare results across the two languages. Also working at a level of fine detail, Su and Huang are concerned with the acquisition of aspects of phonology: awareness at the levels of phoneme, intrasyllabic unit and syllable; they designed tests in which participants attempted to discriminate sounds at these levels.

Like Benati and Romero-López and Su and Huang, Ife looks at the acquisition of a specific linguistic feature, in this case the distinctions in use between the three Spanish verbs *ser*, *estar* and *haber*. She examined the use of these verbs in a corpus of beginner learner writing and found consistent patterns of errors. Although there are some precedents for the use of a corpus of learner writing, Ife's work is original in the application of corpus methodology to beginner learners. Her corpus is organised so that she can trace the source of each citation, and this enables her to find patterns associated with particular first languages, and even with specific coursebooks that some groups of learners have used.

Kobayashi and Rinnert's work is original in its comparison of learners' writing levels in both their L1, Japanese, and target language, English. It is also rich in that the researchers consider both fluency and mastery of textual features, using established measures adapted from research in discourse analysis. An important feature of Williams' work is the development of a tool for investigating motivation, working from her model of motivation, which combines research from psychology and applied linguistics. This leads her to develop scales along which motivation can be described and measured, through the use of interview questions.

Through the fusion of ideas and models from disparate fields within applied linguistics and from other disciplines, and through creative research methodology, the writers in this section have produced a number of useful and thought-provoking findings. Benati and Romero-López claim that the most significant aspect of processing instruction is structured input activities, a finding of importance to teachers concerned with their learners' difficulty in mastering details of structure. Su and Huang confirm the difficulty of English phonology for Chinese learners, and suggest that awareness at the level of syllable is earlier than at other levels. They argue that this finding is significant for the teaching of reading as well as for phonology. Ife shows the importance of the coursebook; learners using coursebooks in which particular structures are under-represented will tend to make more errors in those structures; the coursebook is possibly a more important factor than the structure of the learners' L1. Ife's paper also has implications for the way in which near synonyms are presented to learners.

Kobayashi and Rinnert's research suggests that experience in L1 and in L2 writing interact, the strongest L2 writers being those who are experienced in both L1 and L2 writing. An important implication of this is that L1 writing experience should not be ignored and that it may be helpful for teachers to seek ways of transferring awareness of L1 writing to L2 writing tasks. Williams presents findings about motivation, a factor underlying all aspects of language learning. She claims that for secondary pupils in Britain, younger learners seem more highly motivated than older, girls more motivated than boys, and pupils in general more motivated to learn German than French. These findings raise interesting questions about the nature of language teaching, and about British culture and attitudes more widely.

If the second group of papers represented perhaps a turn back to language teaching and learning, the third group of papers represents the 'social turn' in applied linguistics research, focusing on the interface between social contexts and language use. The contexts range in scope and focus from a hostile email communication between members of a business ethics discussion group, pupil/teacher interaction in an Athens primary school, football commentating in Hong Kong, and English use in Africa, but in all the papers, there is a concern to interrogate the ways in which language and society work in relation to each other, in areas such as the creation and expression of professional relationships, the implications of language use for issues of individual and national identity, and the investigation of real-life institutional and cultural practices from a linguistic perspective. The writers use the tools of linguistics, such as phonology and conversation analysis, to examine language use, whilst at the same time considering the influence of societal factors such as ethnicity, identity and social status on the language events within the contexts which they describe.

Rubagumya, in considering the role which English plays within globalisation processes as they are currently affecting Africa, addresses the complex inter-relationship between language use and political and social development. Many researchers have assumed that English shapes these types of development, either positively (e.g. Bisong, 1995) by helping Africans to become equal partners in the globalisation process alongside more wealthy English-speaking countries, or negatively, (e.g. Phillipson, 1992) by positioning them as the clients and consumers for such countries. Rubagumya turns this argument on its head by suggesting that English use is a result of globalisation rather than a cause. He argues that English has failed to help Africans to acquire the skills and capital needed to enter the global market, since access to English is confined to a small elite. Whilst he does not dismiss the usefulness of English for external communication, he proposes that economic power for African states may be achieved through regional integration and the use of African regional languages, rather than attempting to use English as a means of entry to a global market, an attempt which will always tend to marginalise the majority of Africans.

Smith's paper is also concerned with the consequences of English use in a context in which it is not a first language, but where it is the original language of an imported cultural practice, English Premier League football. He explores the problems faced by football commentators in Hong Kong in translating the names of English football teams, and in doing so illuminates a number of issues which confront translators in reaching decisions about equivalence. Most of the translations represent attempts to find phonetic representations in Cantonese which are as close as possible to the original sounds in the names of the English teams, but the lack of fit between the Cantonese and English sound systems results in interesting substitutions and additions to sounds, particularly in the case of tones, certain fricatives and consonant clusters. Care also needs to be taken to avoid sounds which might have unfortunate connotations in Cantonese. Elsewhere, there are teams whose names are represented semanti-cally rather than phonetically, so that Wolverhampton Wanderers, or 'Wolves', is translated as 'wolf pack' in Cantonese. Smith says that 'the problems of soccer commentators [in finding translational equivalents in Cantonese for English names] may seem rather unimportant, but they do have considerable significance for other more serious issues'. English brand names, the names of geographical locations and prominent people amongst many other such items are currently being translated into a large number of other languages, and the decisions and problems faced by translators in this context are replicated widely elsewhere.

Lytra's paper makes a valuable contribution to our understanding of how language use within the classroom permits teachers and students to present a number of differing social identities. She considers the role of 'play frames' such as teasing and joking, which can occur within the context of whole class instruction and draws on insights from interactional sociolinguistics and conversation analysis in order to explore the functions of both teacher-led and pupil-initiated shifts to play frames. She finds that while teachers tend to limit their own participation in play frames to single turns, they exploit such frames strategically for the purposes of assessment and reproof. Frame shifts to play also allow both pupils and teachers to foreground non-institutional identities within the classroom context. Teachers, by introducing the 'voices' of peers or carers in play frames, have the opportunity to enrich their interpersonal relationships with their pupils, while at the same time preserving their identity and role as controllers of what happens within the classroom. Pupils, by resisting teacher-led attempts to switch back from play to instruction, or by initiating play frames themselves, construct themselves as active participants in classroom discourse, with opportunities to present an alternative interactional order to that put forward by the teacher and to express gender and peer group ties which are more commonly found outside the classroom.

The final paper considers perhaps the smallest and most homogeneous context in terms of participants. We have moved, over the four papers in this section, from the wide geographical reach of language use in the whole of Africa, to focus on a single email discussion on the topic of Business Ethics, which occurred on a public, unmoderated discussion list, and which gave rise to hostile exchanges between the participants. Email has often been referred to as a mixed genre, which shares some of the discoursal features of both written and spoken language (e.g. Yates, 1993). Harrison focuses on aspects of the interaction between the email participants which appear to resemble repairs in conversation, and uses the tools of conversational analysis to do so. She compares instances of genuine email repairs with the examples of apparent repairs or initiations for repair which are found in the hostile discussion, which are in fact used to fan the flames of acrimony rather than to overcome problems in the interaction. Harrison makes the interesting suggestion at the end of her paper that such 'pseudo-repairs' may in fact happen in hostile face-to-face conversations too, and that this is an area which is relatively unresearched. Thus research into how repairs work in one genre, emails, can suggest a new perspective on how they may work within another genre.

References

Bartholomae, D. (1985) Inventing the university. In M. Rose (ed.) *When a Writer Can't Write.* New York: Guilford Press.

Bisong, J. (1995) Language choice and cultural imperialism: a Nigerian perspective. *English Language Teaching Journal* 49(2): 122–32.

Ellis, R.J. (2003) *Interdisciplinarity* http://www.lang.ltsn.ac.uk/resources/goodpractice.aspx?resourceid=1430#relatedresources Accessed 11/5/2004.

Goswami, U. and Bryant, P. E. (1990) *Phonological Skills and Learning to Read.* London: Erlbaum.

Ivanic, R. (1998) *Writing and Identity: the discoursal construction of identity in academic writing.* Amsterdam: Benjamins.

Jones, C., Turner, J. and Street, B. (1999) *Students Writing in the University: cultural and epistemological issues.* Amsterdam: Benjamins.

Latour, B. (1987) *Science in Action: how to follow scientists and engineers through society.* London: Harvester Wheatsheaf.

Lea, M. and Stierer, B. (eds) (2000) *Student Writing in Higher Education: new contexts.* Buckingham: Society for Research into Higher Education and Open University Press.

Lillis, T. (2001) *Student Writing: access, regulation, desire.* London: Routledge.

Phillipson, R. (1992) *Linguistic Imperialism.* Oxford: Oxford University Press.

Prior, P. (1998) *Writing/Disciplinarity: a sociohistoric account of literate activity in the academy.* Mahwah, NJ: Lawrence Erlbaum.

Sarangi, S. and van Leeuwen, T. (2003) (eds) *Applied Linguistics and Communities of Practice.* London: British Association for Applied Linguistics in association with Continuum.

Yates, S. (1993) The textuality of Computer-Mediated Communication: speech, writing and genre in CMC discourses. PhD thesis, Milton Keynes: The Open University.

2 The agonism and the ecstasy: conflict and argument in applied linguistics

Richard Badger

University of Leeds

Abstract

Conflict and argument are important elements in the development of academic discourses (Hunston, 1993). However, Tannen (2002) argues that agonism, or ritualized adversativeness, is a source of 'obfuscation of knowledge and personal suffering' (2002: 1651). This paper describes an investigation into agonism in applied linguistics using a corpus of four sets of three articles, where the sets are made up of an original article, a response and a reply to that response by the author or authors of the original article. The paper presents some evidence for saying that extended arguments lead to a focus on boundaries between disciplines and sub-disciplines and also that the arguments become more personal as they go on.

Introduction

Conflict and argument are important elements in the way academic disciplines develop (Hunston, 1993; Popper, 1972; Seidlhofer, 2003). This approach to disciplinary development encourages critical and reflective ways of thinking among the disciplinary community and is one of the mechanisms by which new ideas are tested before they become part of the cultural capital of the disciplinary community. The discourse in which this development is discussed often draws on the metaphor that argument is war (Lakoff & Johnson, 1980), revealed in language such as:

> Linguistics is arguably the most hotly contested property in the academic realm. It is soaked with the blood of poets, theologians, philosophers, philologists, psychologists, biologists, and neurologists, along with whatever blood can be got out of grammarians. (Fauconnier & Turner, 2002)

The war metaphor can, potentially at least, have detrimental effects on the ways in which argument is conducted and Tannen identifies one particular kind of argument, ritualised adversativeness or agonism, as:

> the source of both obfuscation of knowledge and personal suffering in academia (Tannen, 2002: 1652)

Tannen (1998; 2002) enumerates a list of negative effects, including an unwillingness to admit that opposing arguments may have strengths, the creation of false or oversimplified dichotomies and says agonism makes it:

> almost impossible for public policy to be influenced by academic research (Tannen, 2002: 1658)

Argument has always played an important role in academic discourse but there are signs that it is being encouraged by developments in academic publishing. Several journals have created sections devoted to arguments between groups of academics. *ELTJ* has recently introduced a section named 'Forum':

> In this section we present contrasting views on a topic of current interest. The first article is one that has been reviewed by the Editorial Advisory Panel and accepted for publication; the second is a commissioned response, to which the author of the original article is invited to make a brief reply. (Bruton, 2002a)

Similarly:

> *Lingua* is introducing a series of provocative articles under the general heading of Lingua Franca. We invite essays of about 2000 words on a favourite topic, voicing strong opinions supported by arguments in an entertaining way. ... Where someone is an obvious target of a particular contribution, he or she will be sent a copy and invited to respond, probably in the same issue of the journal. (Borsley & Ingham, 2002)

All these developments suggest there is a need to follow Tannen's advice that:

> we who have made a vocation of understanding language in context should be attuned to how the agonistic conventions driving our own discourse are affecting both the scientific understanding that, I continue to believe, is our primary goal, and the human community of which we are a part (2002: 1667)

Some research questions

Despite the importance and frequency of argument in academic discourse generally and specifically in Applied Linguistics, the literature in this area is limited (Hunston, 1993; Seidlhofer, 2003; Tannen, 1998; 2002). One of the reasons for this is the methodological difficulty in firstly deciding what counts as an argument or conflict and then secondly assessing whether or not a particular argument leads to a development in the discipline or what its influence might be on the members of a particular disciplinary community.

In this paper I am making some preliminary suggestions as to:

- what data we might use to investigate arguments;
- how we might then analyse the data to find out if the argument leads to, firstly, disciplinary development or obfuscation and, secondly, increased solidarity within the disciplinary community or personal suffering.

Some data or what counts as an argument

This paper examines a particular kind of written argument that is realised in the form of series of articles. The study looks at four such arguments, represented in a corpus of 12 academic articles in sets of three, where the argument is initiated by the first author or authors, another author or authors respond and finally the original author or authors provides some feedback. In two cases the argument appeared in a section of a journal devoted to such disputes, which I term commissioned argument and in two cases the argument was spontaneous:

Six from *Applied Linguistics* (spontaneous disagreement) (Aston, 1995; G. Cook, 2001; 2003; V. Cook, 2002) (Lightbown, 2002a; 2002b; Sheen, 2002);

Three from *ELTJ* (commissioned disagreement) (Bruton, 2002a; 2002b; Skehan, 2002);

Three from *Lingua* (commissioned disagreement) (Borsley & Ingham 2002; Borsley & Ingham, 2003; Stubbs, 2002).

The terminology is borrowed from the analysis of classroom discourse (Coulthard, 1985) with the first article labelled initiation, the second article response and the third feedback. The labels are largely a matter of convenience but they serve to make the point that the original author(s) are generally allowed to conclude the argument and this can mean that those who play the first move in the conflict are in a stronger position than those who respond.

Table 1 gives details of the authors, the numbers of words in the articles and in the corpus as a whole.

	Borsely Ingham & Stubbs	Bruton Skehan	Cook & Cook	Lightbown & Sheen	Total
Initiation	2333	3923	9703	12 659	28618
Response	1759	3454	3134	3898	12245
Feedback	1374	428	2812	2691	7305
	5466	7805	15649	19 248	48168

Table 1 Numbers of words in the articles, excluding list of references

The articles get shorter as the argument continues but there are differences in the rate of reduction. This may be a reflection of the policy of the particular journal, a view that is supported by the fact that the two Applied Linguistics arguments display fairly similar patterns of reduction. The most marked reduction occurs in Bruton and Skehan and it may be that here it reflects a feeling that the argument has reached some kind of a conclusion.

We now turn to a consideration of the extent to which the arguments contribute firstly to developments in the discipline (which I would see as approximating to the Hallidayan field) and secondly to interpersonal solidarity (which I would relate to Hallidayan tenor). Each article manifests a balance between arguments about the discipline and about personalities and so I have organised the rest of the paper into three sections. The first looks at the balance between these two aspects and the second and third sections look at disciplinary developments and the solidarity of the disciplinary community, respectively.

The approach relies heavily on a corpus based approach (Hunston, 2002; Partington, 2003) and is intended to offer some indication of possible concordance based research methodologies.

The balance between the discipline and the personalities

I investigated the balance between field and tenor by using the keywords facility on Wordsmith (Scott, 1999). The keywords in a text are those that appear more frequently in the text than in some larger corpus and so give some indication of the most salient vocabulary in each text. Here I compared the words used in each article with a 50,000 word corpus of articles taken from a random selection of non-argument articles in *System, Applied Linguistics, Language and Education, Linguistics and Education, Lingua* and *ELTJ*. Tables 2 to 5 give the keywords for the argument articles and Table 6 gives the keywords for three non-argument articles chosen at random from *Language and Education* and *Linguistics and Education*. If there were more than ten words only the first ten have been included.

BI (Initiation)	Stubbs	BI (Feedback)
Borsley	BI	Stubbs
Ingham	Corpus	We
Graddol	Linguistics	Linguistics
Stubbs	Sinclair	Mainstream
Lingua	Work	Linguists
Linguistics	Francis	Intuitions
	Linguists	He
	Theoretical	That
	Applied	Kress
	Mainstream	Graddol

Table 2 The first ten keywords in BI and Stubbs argument

Bruton (Initiation)	Skehan (Response)	Bruton (Feedback)
Tasks	Tasks	TBI
Task	Task	Pre[task]
Oral	Bruton	Proponents
PW (Pair Work)	Learners	
GW (Group Work)	Approach	
Syllabuses	LA	
Assimilation	Language	
Types	Naturalistic	
Synthetic	Focus	
PPP		

Table 3 The first ten keywords In Bruton and Skehan argument

G.Cook	V. Cook	G.Cook
Sentences	Invented	Vivian
Invented	Attested	Argument
Sentence	IS (Invented Sentences)	Cook
Guy	Examples	IS
Memorable	Sentences	Cook's
Cook's	Bizarre	Evidence
Elements	Cook	Conscious
Example	Sweet	Wording
Conscious	Oxford	Subconscious
Cook	Invention	Sentences

Table 4 The first ten keywords in Cook and Cook argument

Lightbown	Sheen	Lightbown
Research	Lightbown	Sheen
SLA (Second Language Acquisition)	SLA	Lightbown
	Research	SLA
Which	She	Research
French	Focus	That
Teachers	Long's	Sheen's
Learners	Generalization	Critique
Feedback	AL (Applied Linguistics)	Teaching
Language	Influence	Influenced
Lightbown	Form	Applied
Immersion		

Table 5 The first ten keywords in Lightbown and Sheen article

(Adams, 2003)	(Baynham, 2001)	(Tan, 2003)
Noticing	Narrative	Idea
Reformulations	Literacy	Ideas
Target-like	Her	Tasks
Stimulated	She	Framing
Recall	Writing	Divergent
Treatment	Practices	Task
Second	Baynham	Significant
Forms	As	Aloud
Lapkin	Identity	Convergent
Post	Generic	Adding

Table 6 The first ten keywords in three non-argument articles

The argument articles include more use of researchers' names and in particular of the names of the parties to the argument than the non-argument articles. In the Borsely/Ingham (BI) and Stubbs and the Lightbown and Sheen arguments the names of the opponents are the most important word in the response and feedback articles.

The presence of the names of those involved in the argument in the list of keywords can be seen as an indication that the argument is a conflict of personalities, and the presence of terms related to argument as an indication of a conflict of ideas. On this basis the BI and Stubbs and the Lightbown and Sheen arguments are more to do with personal differences. In contrast, the Cook and Cook – and especially the Bruton and Skehan arguments – are more to do with ideas and so less likely to impact on the solidarity of the disciplinary community. A more detailed analysis of the ways the writers refer to their opponents is offered in the section 'Argument and the disciplinary community' below.

Developments in the field

A reading of the set of the articles suggested that there was very little evidence of development within the field. So, for example, it would be hard to see that the importance of tasks in ELT methodology has been altered by the exchange of views, and comments from the authors of several of the articles confirms this. This is probably mainly due to the limited amount of data examined in this study and a much large data set collected over a much longer period of time would probably be needed to address this issue. However, the structure of this kind of argument may also be a contributory factor in the apparent lack of development. By setting up the argument as a dialogue in which the same person has the opening and closing move, the editors of these journals have made the possibility of an agreed outcome to the argument very unlikely. It would be interesting to see what would happen if the editors required that the final argument, the feedback in my terms, had to be written jointly by both sets of authors.

The approach adopted here is to treat these arguments as sites for the possible microgenesis of developments in the discipline (Lantolf, 2000). What follows identifies the central ideas in the articles based on the keyword analysis and examines how the writers deal with these ideas as an indicator of possibilities for disciplinary development (see Tables 6 and 7).

BI & Stubbs	Bruton & Skehan	Cook & Cook	Lightbown & Sheen
BI	Tasks	Sentences	SLA
Corpus	Task	Invented	Research
Linguistics	PW (Pair Work)	IS (Invented	Lightbown
Sinclair	GW (Group Work)	Sentences)	That
Work	PPP	Cook	Language
		Vivian	

Table 7 The first five keywords in each argument

The keywords, which do not refer to participants in the argument, provide an indication of the ideas, which are being contested. In what follows I provide a detailed analysis of the BI and Stubbs argument and, for reasons of space, summary analyses of the other articles.

Borsely, Ingham and Stubbs

In the BI and Stubbs argument the first keyword is 'corpus' which I have taken to mean corpus linguistics on the basis that the second relevant item is linguistics. If we separate statements which report other people's views (8 and 9 in Table 8) from those that implicitly or explicitly give BI's opinions. Where they are expressing their own views BI take a fairly even-handed approach to 'corpus', with four negative collocations (1, 2, 3, 4) as against three positive collocations (5, 6, 7).

Negative points about corpus linguistics

1. Another *problem* with a **corpus** is that it is difficult to conclude anything from the fact that some type of example does not appear in it.
2. A **corpus** is *just* a collection of sounds or marks on a surface.
3. Hence the only way to find out about meanings is to ask native speakers. Anyone who doubts this should try analyzing a **corpus** of speech or writing from a language that they do not know without the help of a native speaker.
4. One is that a **corpus** is only as useful as one's ability to search it.

Positive points about corpus linguistics

5. **Corpus** data is also central in work on the early stages of child language.
6. Moreover, there is obviously no alternative to **corpus** data if the speakers are dead.
7. Hence, mainstream work on dead languages is inevitably based on a **corpus** (supplemented by intelligent guesses about meanings).

Other people's view of corpus linguistics

8. Stubbs, Graddol and others see a **corpus** of speech or writing as a *better* source of data than intuitions.
9. Applied linguists who advocate reliance on a **corpus** have *failed to appreciate the limitations* of such a methodology.

Table 8 'Corpus' in BI's initiation

In the response (Stubbs, 2002), eight out of 19 of the author's comments about corpus linguistics relate to other people's, and in particular BI's, views of corpus linguistics (see Table 9). Three statements can be interpreted as positive about corpus linguistic and two statements can be classified as negative or at least recognising the limits of the corpus approach (statements 12 and 13). There are four statements addressing the issue of whether corpus linguistics is pure or applied. This aspect of the argument concerns what counts as linguistics and is less likely to lead to new developments in (applied) linguistics.

BI's view of corpus lingustics

1. BI point to areas where debate is certainly needed, but this debate must be based on an accurate assessment of (1) the intensive discussions within Applied Linguistics since the 1970s; (2) the *foundational* work in **corpus** linguistics, and (3) approaches to meaning as use.
2. Throughout their article, BI wrongly identify Applied Linguistics with text and **corpus** analysis.
3. Borsley and Ingham (2001, henceforth BI) criticize Applied Linguistics and **corpus** linguistics, and contrast these two areas with what they repeatedly call 'mainstream' linguistics.
4. But it is misleading to imply that **corpus** studies are restricted to lexis.
5. I do not know of any work in **corpus** linguistics (or anywhere else) which tries to make a coherent object of study out of properties of texts such as BI propose: 'being interesting, being libellous'.
6. BI say that 'a **corpus** is only as useful as one's ability to search it'.
7. BI then make two very misleading statements about **corpus** work.
8. We come therefore to one area which BI criticize: computer-assisted **corpus** linguistics.

The advantages of corpus linguistics

9. Some of the most important methods and concepts are illustrated with *detailed grammatical examples* by Hunston and Francis (1999), two scholars who have played a leading role in producing **corpus**-based dictionaries and grammars.
10. Many patterns, particularly concerning connotations, are not recorded in pre-**corpus** dictionaries.
11. The collocational patterns are not derivable from single instances (invented or attested), but *only from repeated instances* across a **corpus** (Sinclair, 1991: 69ff).

The limits of corpus linguistics

12. The empirical findings and theoretical claims of **corpus** study must be tested by looking seriously at the best descriptions and theoretical statements available.
13. It is unnecessary to demand **corpus** evidence for such facts.

Is corpus linguistics pure or applied?

14. Some linguists apply **corpus** methods to real-world problems, such as authorship attribution (e.g. in forensic linguistics).
15. Many applied linguists make no use of text and **corpus** analysis.
16. Much **corpus** work is not applied at all.
17. Conversely, many **corpus** linguists have purely *theoretical* aims of describing and understanding how language is organized.

Questions about corpus linguistics

18. Why not take substantial and innovative '**corpus**-driven' grammars (e.g. Francis et al., 1996;1998) and evaluate their empirical findings and their implications for grammatical theory?
19. Why not contrast and relate evidence from different sources: introspective data (from the linguist her/himself), elicited data (from experimental subjects) and corpus data (randomly sampled from large numbers of speakers)?

Table 9 'Corpus' in Stubbs' response

Stubbs also makes two proposals which might help to evaluate the merits or corpus linguistics and this can be seen as providing a space in which the discipline of (applied) linguistics might develop.

Table 10 gives some information about BI's feedback. The number of references to other people's views about corpus linguistics and to BI's original statements about corpus linguistics form the majority of the comments with only four comments making points about corpus linguistics itself.

Other people's views of BI's views of corpus linguistics

1. In Stubbs (2001) he remarks that his **corpus** 'shows a strong tendency for GET-passives to be used for talking about unpleasant events' (2001: 164).
2. When he is not misrepresenting us, he is mainly engaged in advertising the kind of **corpus**-based work that he is interested in.
3. Rather he devotes himself to criticizing us for positions we did not advocate and to advertising the kind of **corpus**-based linguistic research that he is interested in.
4. Thus, Teubert et al. (2001) assert that we claim that 'Michael Stubbs . . . suggests that **corpus** linguists know more about the production of texts such as the Declaration of Independence.'

BI's views of corpus linguistics

5. We do not identify Applied Linguistics with text and **corpus** analysis or anything else.
6. He suggests that we 'identify Applied Linguistics with text and **corpus** analysis', but we make it clear that we are concerned with the views of 'some applied linguists'.

Positive comments about corpus linguistics

7. The second author has in fact done extensive **corpus**-based work in the acquisition of syntax and diachronic syntax (see Ingham, 1998; 2000).
8. We would like to stress, however, that we have no objection to **corpus**-based linguistic research.

Negative points about corpus linguistics

9. If he were a monolingual speaker of Russian, he could stare at the **corpus** for ever and he would not know anything about how GET-passives are used.
10. However, we took Stubbs (1996) to be arguing that intuitions are a disreputable kind of data and we quoted two remarks which appeared to be saying this. We were concerned to show that they are in fact indispensable (a) because it is impossible to search a **corpus** for many things that mainstream linguists are interested in, (b) because it is difficult to conclude anything from the absence of a certain sort of example from a **corpus**, and (c) because it is impossible to find out about meanings without using intuitions.

Table 10 'Corpus' in BI's feedback

The increasing number of statements related to views of corpus linguistics rather than corpus linguistics itself suggests that this kind of argument has limited value for the development of the field. The limited evidence provided here suggests that the longer such arguments go on the more they focus on the participants rather than the topic.

Bruton and Skehan

The keywords were 'task', 'tasks' and 'TBI' (Task Based Instruction). There were 90 instances of the two words in the first article (Bruton, 2002a), which I classified on an intuitive basis as 42 neutral, 41 negative and seven positive towards the use of tasks. Some examples would be:

> Some use of the Ll is admitted in classroom tasks (Willis, 1996), while projects completed outside the classroom are more difficult to monitor in terms of the oral language used. (Neutral)

> The subjects who interacted in groups in order to complete the tasks were outperformed by those who did not interact at all. (Negative)

> The second reason is that PW/GW tasks can encourage collaborative classroom activity. (Positive)

The response (Skehan, 2002) included 93 mentions of task(s). Fifty-five of these are positive, 24 are neutral, 12 refer, generally negatively, to Bruton's opinions of task and two are negative:

> Structured tasks and tasks based on familiar information are more likely to produce higher accuracy. (Positive)

> SLA researchers have tended to formalize what they were doing, and to speak increasingly not of activities but of tasks. (Neutral)

> Bruton misrepresents language learning tasks. (Bruton's views)

> A possible slight problem is that research into tasks tends not to be on a 'grand scale', but instead is more focused, attempting to discover fundamental aspects of tasks which have an impact. (Negative)

The relatively high number of neutral statements may indicate that this argument is more to do with whether or not task based approaches are useful rather than personal disagreement. In some ways the following sentence summarises Skehan's argument:

> We do not have complete solutions yet, so the key issue is to decide how we can make progress, and add to what we know about tasks, rather than dismiss them because we do not yet have the whole story.

In the final article in the argument (Bruton, 2002b) mentions task, tasks or TBI nine times. Three of these refer to Bruton's comments in the first article and the remainder are negative statements about tasks. Some examples follow:

> I still maintain that TBI proponents, in their zeal, have overshot the mark. (Bruton's earlier comments)

> These support tasks are very often deadly boring, and may not ensure assimilation or transfer, either. (Negative)

The first statement is a reasonable summary of Bruton's position and, taken with Skehan's earlier admission about the lack of complete solutions, makes it clear that the argument is not about abandoning tasks but the extent to which task based approaches lead to learning. It is possible to put forward the hypothesis that this argument is more likely to lead to developments in the field than the BI and Stubbs article.

Cook and Cook

The keywords here were sentence(s), or IS(s) (an abbreviation for Invented Sentences).

The initiation (G. Cook, 2001) uses the key terms 134 times. This article is much more clearly positioned as part of an on-going debate than the other spontaneous argument. So we find the expected statements in favour of invented sentences (37) against (22) and neutral (21) but we also have 31 instances of other people's, generally negative, views being reported, with another seven instances of comments on those views. We also have a set of 16 instances where Cook makes meta-discoursal comments about the text:

> The IS remained the mainstay of graded structural approaches. (Positive)

> He argued (Firth, 1968: 175) that the IS is meaningless. (Other people's negative views)

> It would be wrong to suppose, however, that in doing this, I am supporting either *the kind* of IS, or *the way* in which it was used in the past. (Meta-discoursal)

The response (V. Cook, 2002) includes 33 instances of sentence, sentences, IS and ISs. Five of these relate to Guy Cook's views, one is a positive comment about invented sentences and two are negative comments about invented sentence. Of the remainder, two discuss definitions of invented sentences, four relate to the views of other commentators on invented or other sentences and 19 deal with the new point of what is learnt or illustrated by invented sentences:

Guy Cook's argument is about the content of the sentence message rather than about the linguistic elements that the student is supposed to learn. (G. Cook's views)

Memorable, interesting, invented sentences may lead to better conscious learning of language and ultimately to better unconscious language use. (Positive comment)

The student's memory of the Tony Oxley sentence shows the pitfalls of remembering the sentence but forgetting the linguistic point. (Negative comment)

A starting point is to quibble slightly over what an invented sentence actually is. (Definitions)

Some people have suggested single-instance learning in which one sentence leads to acquisition of a grammatical rule (Nelson, 1981). (Other commentators' views)

It is the language elements the student is eventually learning, not the meaning of particular sentence. (What is learnt)

This is evidence of a lack of engagement between the two authors. Guy Cook raises issues about the prohibition of invented sentences whereas Vivian Cook is concerned with what is learnt from these and other sentences.

This lack of engagement is also reflected in the final article in this argument (G. Cook, 2003) which uses 'sentence(s)' 11 times, of which six are in statement's related to Vivian Cook's earlier statements and five are to do with the nature of language learning.

Is it true, though, that the only significant function of examples is to act as a vehicle for grammatical structures to enter into the subconscious processing mechanisms of the mind? Aptly enough, Vivian Cook uses a culinary metaphor to claim that it is. (V. Cook's views)

What is it that students learn in learning English (or any other language), and how do example sentences help them to do so? (The nature of language learning)

The low number of mentions of 'sentence(s)' suggests that the topic of the argument has moved on from a discussion of the role of invented sentences.

Lightbown and Sheen

Here the keywords were 'SLA' and 'research' so I prepared concordances for 'SLA research' The first article (Lightbown, 2002a) included 59 uses of 'SLA research', 21 of which were neutral, 24 positive and 14 negative. Sheen's (2002) response has 34 uses of 'SLA research', three of which are positive, eight of which are negative and 23 of which relate to Lightbown's views. However, many of the comments on Lightbown's views relate to whether SLA/Applied Linguistics had a significant influence on language learning and teaching in the 1970s and 1980s, where Sheen holds that there was such an influence and Lightbown holds there was not. This disagreement is less factual than to do with boundaries and, rather as BI and Stubbs disagreed about the relationship and boundary between applied and other kinds of linguistics, so Lightbown and Sheen disagree about whether SLA and Applied Linguistics are one or two disciplines. This issue is picked up in the final article (Lightbown, 2002b) where out of 22 mentions, seven relate to the separation between SLA and Applied Linguistics. This compares with the perhaps surprising nine negative comments, three neutral and one each of positive comments, comments about Sheen's views and Lightbown's own views as laid out in the first article.

The debate about the relationship between SLA and Applied Linguistics is important but the shifting of ground means that it is less likely that this debate will lead to developments in the field.

Argument and the disciplinary community

This section examines the impact of argument on the disciplinary community focusing particularly on the authors of the articles. The first kind of analysis relates to the number of times the authors refer to the other author(s) involved in the argument.

The number of references to the other authors varies between the sets of articles, and I would suggest that the number of references to the other authors reflects the level of solidarity between the two sides of the article with fewer references indicating more solidarity. There are also differences in whether the final article has more or fewer references to opponents than the second. So the BI and Stubbs, and Cook and Cook article have the highest number of references in the final article.

The conventions of academic writing restrict the use of the interpersonal resources of the language and so the relations between the parties are largely signalled through the ideational system. To investigate this I examined those sentences where the opposing author or authors is an agent (Halliday, 1994) and analysed the verbal processes. The results of this analysis are given in Tables 11 to 13.

	Borsely & Stubbs		Bruton & Skehan		Cook & Cook		Lightbown & Sheen	
	n	%	n	%	n	%	n	%
Initiation	8	0.34	9	0.23	0	0.00	0	0.00
Response	26	1.48	16	0.46	17	0.54	68	1.74
Feedback	32	2.33	3	0.70	35	1.24	53	1.97

n = number of occurrences in the text
% = number of occurrences as a percentage of total words in article
References here is the number of sentences including the use of the person's/persons' name and any personal pronouns referring to the other people involved in the argument.

TABLE 11 Number of references to opposing author(s)

	BI on Stubbs	Stubbs on BI	BI on Stubbs
	Initiation	Response	Feedback
Material	0	0	0
Mental	2	8	6
Verbal	3	4	8
Relational	1	0	1
Total mentions	7	12	14

Table 12 References by Borsely/Ingham and Stubbs to each other as agents

	Bruton on Skehan	Skehan on Bruton	Bruton on Skehan
	Initiation	Response	Feedback
Material	1	4	0
Mental	1	3	0
Verbal	0	3	1
Relational	0	0	0
Total mentions	2	10	1

Table 13 References by Bruton and Skehan to each other as agents

In the BI and Stubbs argument the parties typically, and unsurprisingly, conceptualise each other as speakers/writers or thinkers. Generally the verbs used here are neutral (e.g. say) however there were also occurrences of more evaluative terms such as 'criticize' and 'assert'. The interpersonal adjuncts or adverbs used with the verbs are also indicative of a lack of solidarity. So BI report that Stubbs 'has apparently forgotten the role of experiments in science' and Stubbs says, 'throughout their article, BI wrongly identify Applied Linguistics with text and corpus analysis.'

Bruton generally refers to Skehan in textual bibliographic references, which positions Skehan as a researcher. Where Bruton refers to Skehan as an agent he uses relatively neutral verbs with 'admit' in the feedback as possibly the most negative. Skehan refers to Bruton much more than Burton initially refers to Skehan, and Skehan uses a surprising number of material verbs (present, use, take, promote). Skehan also uses some negative verbs (mistake, misrepresent) and does not use any bibliographic references for Bruton, except for one in the list of references at the end of the article. Skehan portrays Bruton not as a researcher, and as more of a practitioner than a thinker.

The Cooks refer to each other much more often as determiners in phrases such as 'Cook's argument', perhaps reflecting the gap between their views. It is also possible that this distance allows the participants to say things such as:

> Guy Cook's admirable essay on the invented sentence sets off hares in all directions. (V. Cook, 2002)

This produces the following response from Guy Cook:

> In his reply to my article on invented sentences (G. Cook 2001), Vivian Cook (2002) begins by referring to it as an 'admirable essay', and immediately 'concedes most of [the] points'. Since, however, he goes on to question its value, it is not easy to see just what either this admiration or concession amounts to! (Cook, 2003)

It would be possible to argue from this that this particular argument has relatively little impact on the solidarity of the disciplinary community. However there is some indication in this article that argument may be more of a reflection of individual style than we have been assuming here. So it is perhaps not surprising that the author of *Language Play, Language Learning* (G. Cook, 2000) should write:

> For food, it certainly makes me glad that Vivian **is** a Cook only by name. (Cook, 2003)

Sheen frequently uses material processes in his depiction of Lightbown (e.g. she 'has so far provided no empirical evidence'). He also includes bibliographic references to her on six occasions. Lightbown primarily treats Sheen as a producer of words. There is one interesting use of a relational verbal process:

> Ron Sheen has a reputation for critiquing research reports.
> (Lightbown, 2002b)

The unusual choice of verb is accompanied by the equally unusual use of the given name, Ron.

Lightbown also uses some fairly negative language about Sheen:

> It is sometimes difficult to understand how Sheen (2002) comes to his interpretations. (Lightbown, 2002b)

> I hope readers will read the original text rather than accept Sheen's interpretation of what is there. (Lightbown, 2002b)

Conclusion

This is a small scale study of argument but it is possible to suggest some conclusions.

Firstly, many of the disputes examined here relate more to question of boundaries between disciplines than to particular developments (BI and Stubbs, Lightbown and Sheen) and also there are often shifts in what is being discussed (Lightbown and Sheen, Cook and Cook). This makes it difficult for the argument to contribute to the development of the discipline and even where there is no boundary dispute and the participants attempt to stay on the same ground, the format of the argument, with only one participant contributing to the final move means that progress is not facilitated.

Secondly there is a tendency for the disputes to become more personal as they go on. This may be a function of the form of the argument and in particular there are some indications that changes in academic publishing may encourage personal conflicts. This is not likely to contribute to the solidarity of the disciplinary community.

References

Aston, G. (1995) Corpora in language pedagogy: matching theory and practice. In G. Cook and B. Seidlhofer (eds) *Principle and Practice in Applied Linguistics: studies in honour of H.G. Widdowson.* 257–70. Oxford: Oxford University Press.

Borsley, R. D. and Ingham, R. (2002) Grow your own linguistics? On some applied linguists' views of the subject. *Lingua* 112(1): 1–6.

Bruton, A. (2002a) From tasking purposes to purposing tasks. *ELT Journal* 56(3): 280–8.

Bruton, A. (2002b) When and how the language development in TBI. *ELT Journal* 56(3): 296–7.

Cook, G. (2000) *Language Play, Language Learning.* Oxford: Oxford University Press.

Cook, G. (2001) The philosopher pulled the lower jaw of the hen. Ludicrous invented sentences in language teaching. *Applied Linguistics* 22(3): 166–87.

Cook, G. (2003) The functions of example sentences: a reply to Vivian Cook. *Applied Linguistics* 245(2): 249–55.

Cook, V. (2002) The functions of invented sentences: a reply to Guy Cook. *Applied Linguistics* 23(2): 262–9.

Coulthard, M. (1985) *An Introduction to Discourse Analysis.* London: Longman.

Fauconnier, G. and Turner, M. (2002) *The Way We Think: conceptual blending and the mind's hidden complexities.* New York: Basic Books.

Hunston, S. (1993) Professional conflict – disagreement in academic discourse. In M. Baker, G. Francis and Tognini-Bonelli (eds) *Text and Technology: in honour of John Sinclair.* 115–36. Amsterdam: John Benjamins.

Hunston, S. (2002) *Corpora in Applied Linguistics.* Cambridge: Cambridge University Press.

Lakoff, G. and Johnson, M. (1980) *Metaphors We Live By.* Chicago: University of Chicago Press.

Lantolf, J. P. (2000) *Sociocultural Theory and Second Language Learning.* Oxford: Oxford University Press.

Lightbown, P. M. (2002a) Anniversary article: classroom SLA research and second language teaching. *Applied Linguistics* 21(4): 431–62.

Lightbown, P. M. (2002b) The role of SLA research in L2 teaching: reply to Sheen. *Applied Linguistics* 23(4): 529–35.

Partington, A. (2003) *The Linguistics of Political Argument: the spin-doctor and the wolf-pack at the White House.* London: Routledge.

Popper, K. R. (1972) *Objective Knowledge: an evolutionary approach.* Oxford: Clarendon.

Scott, M. (1999) *Wordsmith Tools.* (Version 3.00) Oxford: Oxford University Press.

Seidlhofer, B. (2003) *Controversies in Applied Linguistics.* Oxford: Oxford University Press.

Sheen, R. (2002) A response to Lightbown's (2000) anniversary article: classroom SLA research and second language teaching. *Applied Linguistics* 23(4): 519–28.

Skehan, P. (2002) A non-marginal role for tasks. *ELT Journal* 56(3): 289–95.

Stubbs, M. (2002) On text and corpus analysis: a reply to Borsley and Ingham. *Lingua* 112: 7–11.

Tannen, D. (1998) *The Argument Culture: changing the way we argue.* London: Virago.

Tannen, D. (2002) Agonism in academic discourse. *Journal of Pragmatics* 34: 1651–69.

3 The effects of structured input activities and explicit information on the acquisition of gender agreement in Italian and the simple past tense in Spanish

Alessandro Benati and Paula Romero-López

University of Greenwich

Abstract

Processing instruction (VanPatten, 1996; 2002; 2003) is a model of grammar instruction, the effects of which have been investigated in different languages, different contexts and linguistic features (see VanPatten, 2002). It represents an alternative to more traditional approaches to grammar instruction and focus on form. It is an approach that attempts to intervene in the processing strategies that learners use to make form-meaning connections from the input. The findings of the empirical studies carried out on the effects of processing instruction have provided substantial empirical support for this approach and have generated considerable international debate. The present paper examines the results obtained in a parallel study conducted by two researchers investigating the processing of input in Italian and Spanish. Both investigations seek to tease apart the components of the processing instruction approach and determine which one is the causative factor in learners' changing performance.

I. Background

Input processing and processing instruction

Processing instruction (PI) is a new type of grammar instruction that is concerned with learners' awareness of how grammatical forms and structures are acquired. This new pedagogical approach, based on the input processing model (see VanPatten, 1996; 2002; 2003), seeks to intervene in the processes learners use to get data from the input. Input processing is concerned with those psycholinguistic strategies and mechanisms by which learners derive intake from input. Research on input processing has attempted to describe what linguistic data learners attend to during comprehension and which ones they do not attend to, for example what grammatical roles learners assign to nouns or how position in an utterance influences what gets processed.

VanPatten (2002; 2003) has identified two main processing principles:

1. Learners process input for meaning.
2. Learners tend to process the first noun or pronoun they encounter in a sentence as the subject or agent (the first noun principle).

These processing principles seem to provide an explanation of what learners are doing with input when they are asked to comprehend it. As a result of the way learners attend to input data, VanPatten (1996) has developed a new kind of grammar instruction which guides and focuses learners' attention when they process input. This new type of grammar instruction called PI is diametrically opposed to traditional instruction which consists of drills in which learner output is manipulated and instruction is divorced from meaning or communication. PI is a more effective method for enhancing language acquisition as it is used to ensure that learners' focal attention during processing is directed toward the relevant grammatical items and not elsewhere in the sentence. It consists of three basic components:

1. Learners are given explicit information (EI) about a linguistic structure or form;
2. Learners are informed about a particular processing strategy that may negatively affect their picking up of the form or structure during comprehension;
3. Learners are pushed to process the form or structure through structured input activities (SIA). In SIA the input is manipulated in particular ways to push learners to become dependent on form and structure to get meaning.

SIA consists of two broad types:

1. Referential activities are those for which there is a right or wrong answer and for which the learner must rely on the targeted grammatical form to get meaning;

2. Affective structured input activities are those in which learners express an opinion, belief, or some other affective response and are engaged in processing information about the real world.

Research on processing instruction

The effects of PI have been investigated in a variety of studies[1] which are aimed at generalising and measuring the effectiveness of this new approach to grammar instruction, when compared to traditional instruction, in different languages, structures and assessment tasks.

Overall the results from all these studies indicate that PI is more successful than traditional instruction in contributing to the development of learner's interlanguage by enabling learners to practice correct form-meaning connections via interpretation. The results of the PI studies seem also to indicate that the effects of PI are observable in different output tasks and are not limited to sentence-level tasks.

Recent research in PI has sought to establish which component within the PI approach is the causative variable for the positive outcomes of instruction. In order to address this question VanPatten and Oikkenon (1996) carried out a study on the acquisition of the word order and object pronouns in Spanish. In this study the three main components of the PI approach were teased apart and their effects measured. The empirical findings of VanPatten and Oikkenon (1996) study suggest that the success of PI is due to the SIA component which would appear to be the main factor in helping learners to internalize the grammatical system of a target language.

These findings were supported by a partial replication conducted by Benati (2003) on the acquisition of the future tense in Italian, and two additional studies (Farley, 2003 on the acquisition of subjunctive in Spanish; Wong, 2003 on negation and indefinite articles and 'partitives' with *avoir* in French) which provided additional support for the main role played by the SIA component.

Motivation for the present investigation

The empirical findings on the experimental studies investigating the causative variable for the positive effects of PI appear to lend support to the view that indicates that EI plays no important role. Exposure to the input through SIA seems to play the key role in facilitating the processing of the linguistic data. Despite the positive outcomes it was not known whether these findings could be generalised for different linguistic structures with low communicative value and a different processing problem (non-redundancy principle).

In order to address these questions two parallel studies were conducted to measure the relative effects of PI and its components (SIA and EI) on the acquisition of the Italian gender agreement and the Spanish simple past tense (*pretérito indefinido*).

If the results of the two studies proved that SIA can cause equal gains to PI in a different processing problem, different grammatical features with low communicative value, then we would have further evidence that SIA alone, due to its nature, is the main factor responsible for changes in learner performance.

Two different processing problems, which are corollaries of VanPatten's first principle, were investigated. In the case of the Spanish study the so called 'lexical preference principle', VanPatten has argued (1996) that learners tend to rely on lexical items as opposed to grammatical form to get meaning when both encode the same semantic information. Under this principle, learners would assign temporal reference relying on lexical cues and not in verb morphology. In the following sentence containing the simple past tense in Spanish, *ayer visité a mi familia* (yesterday I visited my family), *ayer* and *-é* carry the same meaning, pastness. In this case, learners will normally skip over the morpheme *-é* for past and will rely on the content word *ayer* for getting the same meaning. In addition, the communicative value (see the explanation below for communicative value) of the simple past tense in this type of input sentences is diminished because of its redundancy.

In the case of the Italian study the preference for non-redundancy principle was investigated. According to this principle learners are more likely to process non-redundant meaningful grammatical form before they process redundant meaningful forms. In the case of gender agreement, adjectives in Italian must agree in number and gender with the noun they modify (*la casa bella*). This feature of grammar is often accompanied by an article or a semantic item. This makes the grammatical feature redundant and lower in communicative value.

Communicative value has been defined by VanPatten (1996) as referring 'to relative contribution a form makes to the referential meaning of an utterance and it is based on the presence or absence of two features: inherent semantic value and redundancy within the sentence utterance' (p. 24). In short, like in the examples described above, if meaning can be retrieved elsewhere and not just from the form itself, then the communicative value of the form is diminished. In addition, in the case of the Italian gender agreement, the form does not have inherent semantic value and it does not add any meaning to the utterance.

Research questions

The research questions in both studies were the following:

1. Which of the following factors (EI alone, SIA alone, or PI) is responsible for the gains in performance when effects are measured by an interpretation task on the acquisition of gender agreement in Italian and the *pretérito indefinido* in Spanish?

2. Which of the following factors (EI alone, SIA alone, or PI) is responsible for the gains in performance when effects are measured by a written production task on the acquisition of gender agreement in Italian and the *pretérito indefinido* in Spanish?

II. Method

Participants

Participants were undergraduate students from Greenwich University (62 subjects in total). All students were English native speakers and had not been exposed to any formal instruction on the targeted linguistic features prior to the treatment. Two parallel studies[2] in Italian (31 subjects) and Spanish (31 subjects) were carried out. In each of the two studies participants were split into three groups using a random procedure (see overview of the two experiments in Figure 1). Participants were assigned to one of the three instructional groups: PI group, SIA only group and EI only group. All participants were tested for knowledge of the two linguistic structures prior to the treatment following a pre-test procedure.

In the case of the Italian study the final total of subjects was the following: PI group ($n = 10$), SIA only group ($n = 11$) and EI only group ($n = 10$). In the case of the Spanish study was: PI group ($n = 7$), SIA only group ($n = 16$) and EI only group ($n = 8$).

Random procedure / Pre-test	Instructional period	Post-tests
Three groups formed PI - SIA - EI	Two consecutive days (Italian study)	Post-tests administered: Interpretation task Written production tasks
Pre-tests administered: Interpretation task Written production tasks	One day (Spanish study)	

Figure 1 Overview of the experiments

Instructional treatments

The experiments were carried out in way which would cause the least amount of disruption to the programme of study. Because of this, the amount of time dedicated in both experiments differed as the curricula in both languages also differed. For the purpose of the experiment, the population for the experimental study in Spanish was taught during one teaching session of two hours, whilst in the case of the experiment in Italian, the group was taught over two teaching sessions (two hours each session) over a period of two consecutive days.

In both experiments, participants were split into three groups. The first group received PI (EI about the target feature followed by SIA practice) whereas the other two groups were exposed respectively to its components: SIA only and EI only. In the case of the EI only group explicit explanation was given and repeated. The time left over was devoted to different practice.

The two instructional packets (see samples of activities in Appendix A and B) designed for these studies were balanced in terms of vocabulary, practice time and number of activities. SIA included an equal number of referential and affective activities (see VanPatten, 2002).

Feedback was provided only on the correctness of student's responses. No explanation or feedback about the target features was given. Learners were only told when their interpretations were right or wrong but they did not receive any information as to why.

The teachers involved acted as facilitators during the experiments and made all possible efforts to pay the same amount of attention and show the same enthusiasm across the different treatment conditions.

In the activities developed and used in both experiments VanPatten's processing principles (1996; 2002; 2003) were taken into account in that learners were encouraged to attend to the grammatical markers. Thus, in the case of the study in Italian, nouns and any other reference to gender were removed in the sentences and only the adjective ending encoded gender in the input sentence. In the case of the study in Spanish, temporal adverbs were removed from the input sentences. Instead, students were forced to attend to the past tense forms to encode the meaning. As PI aims at making learners interpret and comprehend the linguistic feature in oral and written form, no activities were developed where learners had to produce the targeted grammatical item.

Assessment tasks

A pre-test and post-test design was used in both studies. Two versions were designed, one served as the pre-test and the other served as the post-test. Pre-tests were administered to the subjects two weeks before the beginning of the instructional period. Post-tests were administered immediately after the end of the instructional period. In both studies two tasks were produced: one interpretation task, one written production task (see a sample in Appendix C and D). All tests were balanced in terms of difficulty and vocabulary in a previous pilot study.

In both investigations, the interpretation tasks aimed at measuring subjects' ability to interpret utterances containing the target structures. The production tasks aimed at measuring the ability to produce the target items. The interpretation tasks contained 10 distracters and 10 target items but only the target items were scored. One point was awarded for a maximum score of 10. The production tasks contained 10 target items and the same system of scoring as in the interpretation task was adopted.

III. Results

Interpretation

The two ANOVAs conducted on the pre-tests of the interpretation tasks in both studies revealed no differences among the three group means before the beginning of the instructional period (in the case of the Italian study $F(2, 31) = 1.404, p = .890$; in the case of the Spanish study $F(2, 31) = .308\ p = .737$).

In both studies a repeated measures ANOVA on the raw scores (pre- vs. post-test) revealed a main effect for Treatment and Time (in the case of the Italian study a main effect for Treatment $F(1, 31) = 262.575, p = .000$, and for Time (pre- vs. post-test), $F(1, 31) = 133.579, p = .000$; in the case of the Spanish study a main effect for Treatment $F(1, 31) = 12.993, p = .000$, and for Time (pre- vs. post-test), $F(1, 31) = 6.529, p = .000$).

Figures 2 and 3 show graphically the improvement from pre-test to post-test for the experimental groups in both studies (means and standard deviations for the interpretation tasks are shown in Table 1). Although the three groups improved from the pre- to the post-test, changes in performance were not all statistically different.

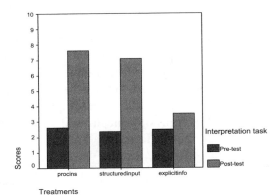

Figure 2 Graphical representation of means (pre-test and post-test) for the interpretation task (Italian study)

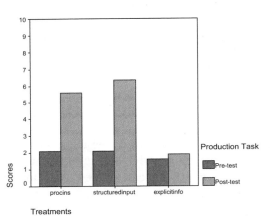

Figure 3 Graphical representation of means (pre-test and post-test) for the written production task (Italian study)

Italian study		Pre-test		Post-test 1	
Variable	N	Mean	SD	Mean	SD
PI	10	2.6	1.1738	7.6	1.1682
SIA	11	2.3	1.2060	7.1	1.0445
EI	10	2.5	.9718	3.5	.9451
Spanish study					
PI	7	2.7	1.1127	7.8	1.5199
SIA	16	2.3	11.955	6.3	1.7078
EI	8	2.5	1.0690	4.0	1.3093

Table 1 Summary of means and standard deviation for interpretation task pre-test and post-test in both studies

In both studies (see the summary of the results in Table 2) a post-hoc Scheffé carried out on post-test results revealed that there was not significant difference between the processing group and the SIA only group, that the PI group performed better than the EI group, and finally that the SIA only group also performed better than the EI group.

Production

Two ANOVAs were also conducted on the pre-tests of the production tasks in both studies. The results revealed no differences among the three group means prior to the start of the instructional period (in the case of the Italian study $F(2, 31) = .894$, $p = .255$; in the case of the Spanish study $F(2, 31) = .336$ $p = .718$).

In both studies a repeated measures ANOVA on the raw scores (pre- vs. post-test) showed again a main effect for Treatment and Time (in the case of the Italian study a main effect for Treatment $F(2, 31) = 81.693$, $p = .000$, and a significant main effect for Time (pre- vs. post-test), $F(1, 31) = 16.620$, $p = .000$; in the case of the Spanish study a main effect for Treatment $F(1, 31) = 27.050$, $p = .000$, and for Time (pre- vs. post-test), $F(1, 31) = 5.679$, $p = .000$).

Figures 4 and 5 show graphically the improvement from pre-test to post-test for the experimental groups in both studies (means and standard deviations for the interpretation tasks are shown in Table 3). Although the three groups improved from the pre- to the post-test, changes in performance were not all statistically different.

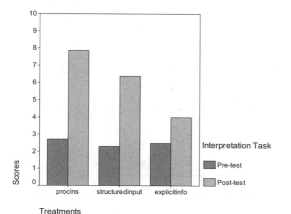

Figure 4 Graphical representation of means (pre-test and post-test) for the interpretation task (Spanish study)

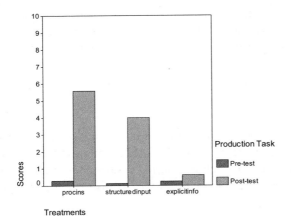

Figure 5 Graphical representation of means (pre-test and post-test) for the written production task (Spanish study)

Studies	Interpretation task	Production task
Italian study	PI=SIA ($p = .648$) PI>EI ($p = .000$) SIA>EI ($p = .001$)	PI=SIA ($p = .110$) PI>EI ($p = .000$) SIA>EI ($p = .004$)
Spanish study	PI=SIA ($p = .583$) PI>EI ($p = .001$) SIA>EI ($p = .000$)	PI=SIA ($p = .088$) PI>EI ($p = .000$) SIA>EI ($p = .000$)

Table 2 Summary of post-hoc findings (post-tests)

Italian study		Pre-test		Post-test 1	
Variable	N	Mean	SD	Mean	SD
PI	10	2.1	.8756	5.6	1.7764
SIA	11	2.09	.7006	6.3	2.1106
EI	10	1.6	.6992	1.9	.7379
Spanish study					
PI	7	0.28	0.4880	5.5	1.5119
SIA	16	0.12	0.5000	4.0	1.7512
EI	8	0.25	0.4629	0.62	0.7440

Table 3 Summary of means and standard deviation for written production task pre-test and post-test in both studies

In both studies (see the summary of the results in Table 2) a post-hoc Scheffé was used on post-test scores. Specifically, the results showed the following contrasts: the PI group was not significantly different than the SIA only group, the PI group performed better than the EI only group and also the SIA only group also performed slightly better than the EI group.

Summary of results

Based on the results presented above, the answers to our research questions are these:

1. The SIA practice seems to be the causative factor in learners' improved performance in the interpretation task. The SIA only group performance was equal to the processing instruction group and superior compared to the EI only group.
2. The SIA practice seems again the main variable responsible for learners' improvement in the production task. Both the PI group and the SIA only group performed better than the EI only group.

IV. Conclusion

The statistical results from both interpretation and production tasks in both studies provide further evidence in a different processing problem (non-redundancy principle) and different structures (Italian gender agreement and Spanish *pretérito indefinido*) with low communicative value, to support the view that it is the SIA practice the main variable for the beneficial effects of instruction within the PI approach. Despite the improved performance of the EI only, the role of EI seems to have a minimal and no significant role. We may conclude that it is the nature of the SIA practice (VanPatten, 2002) which has caused changes in learner performance. The manipulation of input through SIA must have helped learners to make form-meaning connections.

Despite the positive outcomes in both investigations, there are some limitations that further research should address. The first one is related to the relatively small number of subjects who took part in both experiments. Although we did seek to tackle in advance this possible limitation by conducting a parallel study, further research should replicate the study with a larger population.

A second limitation relates to the use of feedback provided to learners in the SIA group. The SIA group received negative feedback during the referential activities which could have acted as a type of EI assisting input processing. If this is the case, then we could conclude that the EI has a role. However, the results from Sanz and Morgan-Short study (2003) on the effects of feedback (explicit and implicit) and EI on the acquisition of Spanish word order could help us to discount this possibility. Their results show that neither explicit information nor explicit feedback had an impact on the performance of the learners.

A third limitation of the present studies is that instructional effects were measured in an immediate post-test only. Hence, the longer-term effects of PI and its components on the acquisition of these particular grammatical features remain to be investigated.

Acknowledgement

We would like to thank the anonymous reviewers for their insightful comments.

Notes

1. (VanPatten & Cadierno, 1993 on Spanish object pronouns; Cadierno, 1995 on Spanish past tense verb morphology; Cheng, 1995 on Spanish copular verbs (*ser* and *estar*); Benati, 2001 on Italian future tense; Farley, 2001 on the Spanish subjunctive; Buck, 2000 on English present continuous; VanPatten & Wong, 2003 on the French *faire* causative; VanPatten & Sanz, 1995 on different amount and mode of tests).

2. Instructional materials and tests are available from the author. For a more detailed description of the two studies see Benati (forthcoming) and Paula Romero-López, 2002.

References

Benati, A. (2001) A comparative study of the effects of processing instruction and output-based instruction on the acquisition of the Italian future tense. *Language Teaching Research* 5: 95–127.

Benati, A. (2003) The effects of structured input activities and explicit information on the acquisition of Italian tense. In B. VanPatten (ed.) *Processing Instruction: theory, research and commentary* (pages forthcoming). Mahwah, NJ: Lawrence Erlbaum.

Benati, A. (forthcoming) The effects of processing instruction and its components on the acquisition of gender agreement in Italian. *Language Awareness.*

Buck, M. (2000) Procesamiento del lenguaje y adquisición de una segunda lengua. Un estudio de la adquisición de un punto gramatical en inglés por hispanohablantes. Unpublished doctoral thesis, Universidad Nacional Autónoma de México.

Cadierno, T. (1995) Formal instruction from a processing prospective: an investigation into the Spanish past tense. *Modern Language Journal* 79: 179–93.

Cheng, A. (1995) Grammar instruction and input processing: the acquisition of Spanish *ser* and *estar*. Unpublished doctoral thesis, University of Illinois: Urbana-Champaign.

Farley, A. P. (2001) The effects of processing instruction and meaning-based output instruction. *Spanish Applied Linguistics* 5: 57–94.

Farley, A. P. (2003) Processing instruction and the Spanish subjunctive: is explicit information needed? In B. VanPatten (ed.) *Processing Instruction: theory, research and commentary* (pages forthcoming). Mahwah, NJ: Lawrence Erlbaum.

Romero-López, P. (2002) Structured input activities or explicit information as main causative variable on the acquisition of Spanish Preterit. Unpublished MA thesis, University of Greenwich: UK.

Sanz, C. and Morgan-Short, K. (in press) Positive evidence vs. explicit rule presentation and explicit negative feedback: a computer assisted study. *Language Learning*.

VanPatten, B. (1996) *Input Processing and Grammar Instruction*. Norwood, NJ: Ablex.

VanPatten, B. (2002) Processing instruction: an update. *Language Learning* 52: 755–803.

VanPatten, B. (2003) Input processing in SLA. In B. VanPatten (ed.) *Processing Instruction: theory, research and commentary* (pages forthcoming). Mahwah, NJ: Lawrence Erlbaum.

VanPatten, B. and Cadierno, T. (1993) Explicit instruction and input processing. *Studies in Second Language Acquisition* 15: 225–43.

VanPatten, B. and Oikkenon, S. (1996) The causative variables in processing instruction: explanation versus structured input activities. *Studies in Second Language Acquisition* 18: 225–43.

VanPatten, B. and Sanz, C. (1995) From input to output: processing instruction and communicative tasks. In F. R. Eckman, D. Highland, P. W. Lee, J. Mileham and R. Weber (eds) *Second Language Acquisition Theory and Pedagogy*. 169–85. Mahwah, NJ: Lawrence Erlbaum.

VanPatten, B. and Wong, W. (2003) Processing instruction and the French causative: a replication. In B. VanPatten (ed.) *Processing Instruction: theory, research and commentary* (pages forthcoming). Mahwah, NJ: Lawrence Erlbaum.

Wong, W. (2003) Processing instruction in French: the roles of explicit information and structured input. In B. VanPatten (ed.) *Processing Instruction: theory, research and commentary* (pages forthcoming). Mahwah, NJ: Lawrence Erlbaum.

Appendix A: Processing instruction

Italian study
Explicit information (sample)

You have probably noticed descriptive adjectives have different gender: in Italian, adjectives must agree in number and gender to the noun they modify.

Masculine = *o*	Feminine = *a*
bello	*bella*
un ragazzo bello	*una ragazza bella*
Clinton è bello	*Claudia Schiffer è bella*

You must pay attention to the adjective ending in order to understand who and what we are referring to. In addition to that, you need to understand the meaning of the sentence containing the adjective.

Sample structured input activity

Listen to each sentence in which a person is described and determine which person is described. Then indicate whether you agree or disagree.

1. ☐ Bill Clinton   ☐ Monica Lewinsky
   ☐ agree   ☐ disagree

2. ☐ Bill Clinton   ☐ Monica Lewinsky
   ☐ agree   ☐ disagree

3. ☐ Bill Clinton   ☐ Monica Lewinsky
   ☐ agree   ☐ disagree

Sentences heard by learner:

1. *È bella*

2. *È dinamico*

3. *È carismatico*

Appendix B: Processing instruction

Spanish study
Explicit information (sample)

Spanish simple past tense is called *pretérito indefinido*. This past tense has different forms from the present tense.

The *pretérito indefinido* serves to report actions, events, and states that are viewed as having been completed in the past.

> Notice that: Past form is usually accompanied by *temporal adverbs* that will indicate that the action has already happened in the past. Here are some of the most common ones: *ayer* (yesterday), *la semana pasada* (last week), *anteayer* (the day before yesterday), *anoche* (last night), etc. However, although these adverbs are a good clue to know that an action has occurred in the past, they are not always present in the sentences. That is why it is very important for you to recognise past tense forms.

THIRD PERSON SINGULAR

Let's see now the third person singular of the regular verbs in the past.

> *El/ ella/ usted . . . se acostó; comió; cenó; salió; habló; vivió*

There are three clues that will help you to recognize the third person singular past verb forms:

1. The past tense (third person) of regular -ar verbs is formed by adding the ending *ó* to the root of the verb, which is obtained by deleting the –ar ending from the infinitive.

2. The past tense (third person) of regular –er, -ir verbs is formed by adding the ending *ió* to the root of the verb, which is obtained by deleting the –er, or –ir endings from the infinitive. Notice that –er and -ir verbs share the same endings, which will be easier for you to remember them.

3. Most of the third person past tense verbs end in a stressed or accented vowel, which is very important to produce, both in oral and written modes. This is crucial in order to distinguish past from the present tense forms (which are unaccented).

Sample structured input activity

<u>¿Quién nació en .....?</u>

Match the number of the name and picture of the following famous Hispanic people with sentences below that indicate where he/she was born (nació en…)

Then, share your answers with your partner giving him/her an opinion as in the exampl

Yo creo que (I think that) Salvador Allende nació en _____

Nació en Chile	Nació en Argentina	Nació en Mé

1. Salvador Allende   2. Cantinflas   3. Evita Perón

Appendix C: Assessment tasks

Italian study

Sample interpretation task

Listen to each sentence in which a person or an object is described and determine which person or object is described.

1. □ Sofia Loren □ Pavarotti
2. □ Birra □ Vino
3. □ Claudia Schiffer □ Brad Pitt

Sentences heard by learner:

1. *È sofisticata*
2. *È buono*
3. *È bionda*

Sample written production task

Fill the gaps with the right adjective agreement. The adjective is provided in brackets!

> *Due volte al mese vado a Milano per lavoro. I miei amici di Roma dicono che è una città (grigi-) _____, ma non è vero. La vita è molto (viv-) _____ e c'è una (bell-) _____ atmosfera. Il posto dove abito è (tranquill-) _____ ma la zona dove lavoro è molto (rumoros-) _____ . C'è un locale che frequento e mi piace molto perchè è (intim-) _____ e c'è un gruppo (divers-) _____ che suona Jazz ogni sera.*
>
> *Milano è una città (modern-) _____ dove si possono incontrare persone da tutto il mondo. Il mio quartiere preferito si trova vicino ai 'Navigli', c'è un ristorante dove vado che non è (car-) _____ e il mangiare è (buon-) _____ .*

Appendix D: Assessment tasks

Spanish study

Sample interpretation task

¿Presente o Pasado? You are going to listen to some sentences in Spanish. Decide whether each sentence you hear has occurred in the present or in the past.

    1. a) Present b) Past

    2. a) Present b) Past

    3. a) Present b) Past

Sentences heard by learner:

    1. *En Londres conoció a su novio*

    2. *Para cenar tomé arroz con pollo*

    3. *En el sur de España se vive muy bien*

Sample written production task

Read the following postcard that Paula writes from Barcelona to her friend Angel. Then complete the sentences in the past with the verbs provided in brackets.

LA SAGRADA FAMILIA.BARCELONA

Hola Angel,
Como ves te escribo desde Barcelona. Es una ciudad
preciosa. Vine el viernes por la tarde a pasar el fin
de semana. Por la noche _____ (salir) a cenar
con unos amigos y lo pasamos muy bien.
El sábado por la mañana _____(visitar) la Sagrada
Familia y me gustó muchísimo. Por la tarde en las
Ramblas _____(cococer) a una chico español
muy simpático y_____(hablar) español con él, se
llama Juan. Al día siguiente _____ (comer)
conmigo en un restaurante del centro de
Barcelona.
Bueno, nos vemos en Londres
Un beso

ANGEL GARCIA

43 Bedford Street

SW5 Londres

---

4 Chinese-speaking children's awareness of English phonological units

Fu-hsing Su[1] and Li-szu Agnes Huang[2]

[1]Department of Foreign Languages,
National Chiayi University, Taiwan

[2]Department of English, Kaohsiung First
University of Science and Technology, Taiwan

Abstract

This study was concerned with Taiwanese children's awareness of English phonological units. Notions from the Developmental Hierarchy Hypothesis were adopted as the theoretical framework. The subjects comprised 186 fifth graders from a Taiwanese elementary school, who took three measures of Phonemic Awareness Test (PAT), Intrasyllabic Awareness Test (IAT), and Syllabic Awareness Test (SAT). These tests evaluated their PA at the phonemic, intrasyllabic, and syllabic levels respectively. Research data were analyzed quantitatively, with the procedures of descriptive statistics and one-way ANOVA observed. The results showed that the subjects scored better for the SAT than the IAT, which in turn out-performed the PAT. There was a significant difference in their performance on the three PA measures. Overall, the relative difficulty for Chinese-speaking children to process English phonological units of different sizes was thus confirmed.

Introduction

This article is concerned with English L2 learners' acquisition of English phonology, specifically with Taiwanese children's awareness of English pho-nological units. The research reported here was motivated by at least two beliefs. First, English PA is a multi-level rather than unitary type of ability or skill. Second, for English L1 children and English L2 children as well, there are different degrees of difficulty in acquiring and processing phonological structures.

Over the past decades, it has been acknowledged that phonological skills are important in explaining variances in the development of linguistic abilities. These abilities are manifested in the domains of speech perception, speech production, pronunciation, word recognition, spelling, etc. Meanwhile, theories have been formulated to account for the progression or rate of acquisition pertaining to phonological development. Researchers have indicated that the development of English Phonological Awareness (PA) is intimately associated with the ability to discriminate sounds at different structural levels. One important topic centering on this development is the relative difficulty of processing constituent units of different structures, i.e., syllables, onsets, rimes, and phonemes.

Purpose of the study

The impetus for the present study came form our attempt to examine the theoretical validity of the Development Hierarchy Hypothesis (DHH). Its hypothetical premises have been adroitly applied to studies or cases where English L1 children were investigated. The applicability of this hypothesis to English L2 children remains uncertain due to inadequate evidence generated by empirical investigations (but see Hu, 1999; 2003; Su, 2003).

Adding to this uncertainty about the validity issue are linguistic differences springing from the internal features of Chinese and English as unique phonological systems. In our opinion, the 'peculiar' characteristics underlying Chinese phonology, as contrasted to those underlying English phonology, are especially distinct in the syllabic and intrasyllabic domains and visible in the phonemic domain. Because of these cross-linguistic differences, it is necessary to pursue empirical confirmation of English L2 children's phonological processing of the Target Language (TL). For this reason, two research questions were posed in the present study: (1) How do Chinese-speaking children perform in PA measures involving syllabic, intrasyllabic, and phonemic units in the target stimuli? (2) Is there relative difficulty for these children to process stimuli involving phonemes, onsets and rimes, and syllables?

Review of literature
Diverse views on English phonological structure

In the literature of English phonology, there has been a convention to designate certain structural units as fundamental to perceptual salience. Earlier work featuring this attempt, such as those by O'Connor and Trim (1953) and Hooper (1972), tended to hold a linear view towards phonological structure. They perceive spoken words as strings of syllables which comprise strings of phonemes. This presumption leads to the conviction that monosyllabic printed words can be parsed into units that correspond to individual phonemes, the smallest phonological unit.

Nonetheless, there are scholars who thought otherwise (Fudge, 1969; Selkirk, 1982). Fudge (1969), for example, proposes an onset-rime structure in English syllables, claiming that most or all phonotactic constraints in English involve two main units: onset and rime. The former refers to the initial consonant or consonant cluster while the latter contains the vowel and any following consonants. For instance, the onset of *peak* is /p/ and that of *train* is /tr/; the rime of *peak* is /ik/ and that of *train* is /en/. Structurally, the rime of an English syllable can be further divided into two parts: the nucleus, which is a mandatory unit, and the coda, which is optional. The coda consists of consonantal sound(s) subsequent to the nucleus. Fudge's notions, despite of their theoretical salience, were unfortunately ignored during the heyday of the linear approach. The customary identification of syllable and phoneme as primary phonological units was largely incontrovertible.

The traditional emphasis on the linear or flat structure of English syllables was largely changed in the late 1980s and early 1990s, when the hierarchical structure view came to light. From then on, researchers started to define the internal structure of English phonology from a fresh perspective. In their remarkable work, Treiman and Chafetz (1987) propose that, internally, spoken syllables have a hierarchical rather than linear structure. Syllables are composed of onsets and rimes, which in turn are composed of smaller units. Drawing evidence from previous work by MacKay (1972), Selkirk (1982), and others, they support the onset-rime division. What they speculate is that written words may have several levels of structure, containing not only units corresponding to syllables but also those corresponding to onsets and rimes.

To gain a clearer picture of the internal phonological structure, Treiman and Chafetz (1987) design two experiments, using an anagram task in Experiment 1 and a lexical decision task in Experiment 2. The anagram task enables the researchers to observe how the subjects segment syllables, as shown in the division of TWIST into TW-IST or TWI-ST and the division of SPREE into

SP-REE or SPR-EE. What they find is that the subjects process TWIST more easily when it is divided into TW-IST rather than TWI-ST. As for the lexical decision task, those stimuli with slashes after the initial consonant letters (e.g., CR//ISP) yield faster response times than the ones with slashes after the vowel (e.g., CRI//SP). These results support the notion that orthographic units corresponding to the onset and rime units of spoken syllables are easier to process.

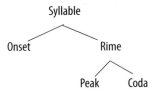

Figure 1 The hierarchical view of syllable structure (Treiman, 1993: 19)

The claims that Treiman and Chafetz (1987) make are in conformity with what Fudge (1969) proposes. Later in another study, Treiman (1993) again advocates theoretical notions of the hierarchical model. She indicates that, other than the traditional division of syllable versus phoneme as the salient processing units, there are intrasyllabic units working as the intermediate agency. The illustration she creates, as shown in Figure 1, best portrays the hierarchical view of English syllable structure.

Notions of the Developmental Hierarchy Hypothesis

Accompanying the hierarchical model is the Developmental Hierarchy Hypothesis, a theoretical paradigm proposed in Goswami and Bryant (1990). The DHH claims that for unilingual English-speakers, there is a hierarchical sequence of the development of PA. As Goswami and Bryant emphasize, three levels of PA are involved in phonological acquisition: syllabic, intrasyllabic, and phonemic levels. Moreover, there is a sequential order of difficulty in acquiring English phonology due to different sizes of structure. As previous studies have shown, awareness of syllable is the earliest or the easiest one to acquire. Learners then develop PA at the intrasyllabic level, realizing that spoken words can share certain beginning properties called onset or ending properties called rime. They finally establish knowledge or awareness of individual phonemes, the smallest unit for sound analysis.

Goswami and Bryant (1990) elaborate on their arguments by putting forward examples of English L1 children acquiring intrasyllabic and phonemic awareness. An important prediction from their theory is that young children should be able to analyze words at the onset-rime level before they can analyze them at the phonemic level. They remark that most children are aware of onsets and rimes (e.g., *train* (/tr/-/ein/) before they are able to analyze and manipulate words as combinations of individual phonemes. The awareness of onset and rime is crucial to the very earliest stages of literacy acquisition. Later Goswami (1993) argue that children who are able to recognize and categories words that rhyme are sensitive to the phonological rime unit. This awareness or sensitivity in turn underpins early reading, allowing them to map sound with spelling at the rime level.

Relative difficulty of processing phonological units

The relative difficulty of processing phonological structures is an issue worth mentioning here, as it has been a topic well documented in the literature of English PA. Remarkably, there is indication that English L1 children's phonological processing starts with syllable as a whole. Earlier researchers unanimously point out that children achieve syllabic awareness much earlier than PA at other levels (Fox & Routh, 1975; Liberman, Shankweiler, Fischer, & Carter, 1974). Ferreiro and Teberosky (1982) propose that children initially believe that writing corresponds to speech at the syllabic level. The syllable is further decomposed into more discrete subsyllabic units and eventually phonemic units. Only later do children realize that the link between print and speech is primarily achieved at the phonemic level.

Discussion on this issue can also be seen in studies by Nittrouer and Studdert-Kennedy (1987) and Nittrouer, Studdert-Kennedy, and McGowan (1989). They further show that English L1 children tend to perceive syllables as relatively undifferentiated wholes. These learners are not as adept as adults at recovering the individual phoneme from the syllable. Their holistic syllabic representation becomes more segmental as their ages advance. Other researchers suggest that, as syllable-initial consonant clusters, onsets are easier to process because they form cohesive units (Bowey & Francis, 1991; Treiman & Zukowski, 1991). More recently, Treiman and Bourassa (2000) note that both early spelling and PA appear to proceed from syllables to units that are intermediate between syllables and phonemes. The connection between spelling and PA arises because performance on both types of tasks reflects the underlying nature of phonological representations. They pinpoint the fact that children's phonological analysis abilities develop further as their exposure to print increases.

Contrastive features underlying Chinese and English phonology

We may balance our views on how English L2 children acquire PA by referring to perspectives from interlanguage phonology. Predictably, English L2 learners' phonological acquisition or development in the TL is juxtaposed with their previous experiences acquiring L1 phonology.

From the view of interlanguage phonology, Chinese and English differ drastically from each other in terms of syllabic structure. Chinese is notoriously known as a language enjoying the prevalent presence of monosyllabic characters and words while there are an enormous number of bisyllabic or polysyllabic items in English. Wang and Smith (1997) remark that Chinese has a very simple syllable structure; it holds CGVC as the maximal syllable structure. Besides the vowel which serves as the core or kernel element of the syllable, all the elements preceding or following the nucleus are basically optional. Ho (1996), a prominent scholar of Chinese phonology, claims that a Chinese syllable consists of two parts: the initial and the final. The initial comprises syllable-initial consonants. The final segments are highly constrained in terms of their categories. Ho characterizes a Chinese syllable as consisting of the following elements.

Initial	Final		
	Glide	Nucleus	Coda

The internal structure of a Chinese syllable constitutes a remarkable contrast to that of an English syllable. This distinction can be defined by a well-formedness template that Harris formalizes (1994, p. 53).

$$[X^3_0]_{onset} [X^2_1]_{nucleus} [X^4_1]_{coda}$$

The maximal inventory of possible syllable types in English is thus impressive. As Harris (1994) calculates, a traditional specification on the set of possible syllabic constituents in English usually runs something like the following. The nuclear part of the rime may contain at least one and at most two positions, as illustrated in *bid* versus *bead*. A maximal of three consonants are allowed to occur syllable-initially and four consonants syllable-finally. The phonotactic sequence underlying English syllable structure is set to be (CCC)V(CCCC).

In the intrasyllabic domain, Chinese and English also differ to a great extent. Lots of Chinese syllables have a zero onset although the majority of Chinese consonants are allowed to occur syllable-initially rather than -finally (Ho, 1996). For each syllable containing an onset, it only allows a maximum number of one consonant and will not take any consonant cluster. Thus in Chinese there are no two-consonant onsets such as /sp/, /st/, /sk/, /sm/, /pl/, /bl/, /tr/, /dr/, etc. or three-consonant onsets such as /spl/, /spr/, /str/, /skl/, /skrl/, /skw/, etc. With regard to rime, there are an enormous number of lexical items that end with an open syllable and contain no coda. As for those syllables which take a coda, only /n/ and /ŋ/ are allowed to occur syllable-finally. It is unimaginable to see two-consonant codas such as /sp/, /st/, /sk/, /mp/, /mt/, /pt/, /kt/, /vd/, /nd/, etc. Likewise, there are no three-consonant codas such as /dst/, /kst/, /mpt/, /mps/, /lpt/, /lkt/, /rkt/, etc. In comparison, the onset and rime structures in English are much more complex than their Chinese counterparts. As Harris (1994) mentions, an English onset can contain between zero and three positions, as illustrated in the word-initial portions of *eye, pie, pry,* and *spry.* The coda part of the rime contains between zero and four positions, as illustrated in the word-final portions of *see* (Ø), *sick* (-k), *six* (-ks), *sixth* (-ksθ), and *sixths* (-ksθs).

As for the phonemic domain, in Chinese voicing is not so functional in making phonetic distinctions as it is in English. The majority of Chinese consonants are voiceless, with the only exceptions of phonemes such as /m/, /n/, /ŋ/, /l/, /ɳ/, and /ẓ/. Next, aspirated and unaspirated sounds in Chinese, unlike their English counterparts, may exist as separate phonemes rather than allophones under the same phonemes. Thus we have independent phoneme pairs of /p/ vs. /pʰ/, /t/ **vs.** /tʰ/, /k/ vs. /kʰ/, /ts/ vs. /tsʰ/, /t$\underline{s}$/ vs. /t$\underline{s}$ʰ/, and /tɕ/ vs. / tɕʰ/. They do not make phonemic contrasts in English. As for vowels, there are also marked differences between the two languages. Wiese (1997) suggests that, in striking contrast to its limited phonotactic possibilities for consonants, Modern Standard Chinese (MSC) allows a number of diphthongs such as /ai/, ei/, /au/, /ou/, /ia/, /ie/, /ua/, /uɣ/, /ye/, etc. There is also a considerable number of triphthongs or a sequence of three vowel sounds within a syllable, such as /iau/, /uai/, /iou/, /uei/, etc.

Experimentally, it is predictable that Chinese-speaking individuals may run into difficulty processing English phonological structures because of the extensive differences between Chinese as their L1 and English as L2. The experiment reported below investigated the effects of English phonological structures on Chinese-speaking children's difficulty in processing these units. Based on the premises from the Developmental Hierarchy Hypothesis, we hypothesized that these learners would demonstrate greater difficulty dealing with phonemes because they required finer-grained analyses. In contrast, they would be more at ease coping with larger structures such as syllables and onsets and rimes.

Methods

Subjects

Subjects of this study comprised fifth graders from an elementary school in the suburban area of Kaohsiung City, southern Taiwan. The original subject size was 186 but the actual number was reduced to 182 after some students dropped out from a specific test. When they participated in this study, they were taking English as a required subject for the first time in the school setting. Their years of learning varied as some of them had previously learned the TL in non-school settings, mainly in private cram schools. They were judged by their respective English instructors and master teachers as learners holding a slim awareness of English phonology.

Research instruments and procedures

Three PA measures of Phonemic Awareness Test (PAT), Intrasyllabic Awareness Test (IAT), and Syllabic Awareness Test (SAT) were administered to the subjects. Each measure aimed to assess the subjects' metalinguistic awareness of phonemes, onsets and rimes, and syllables.

The PAT evaluated the subjects' phonemic awareness or the ability to discriminate individual sounds in a stimulus. The subjects responded to the task by writing down on an answer sheet the number of constituent phonemes in a test item. For example, they needed to indicate 'four' for the test word *dark* and 'three' for *keep,* which consisted of four and three phonemes respectively. To perform well, they had to first perceive then discriminate and eventually identify the individual segments in each auditory stimulus. The PAT comprised three sub-tests wherein a target phoneme occurs in the word-initial, -medial, or -final position, i.e., the /b/ phoneme in *bell, above,* and *job*. There were 22, 24, and 21 test words in the three parts respectively. Due to phonotactic restrictions, there was absence of items containing a specific phoneme in a certain position, as exemplified in word-initial sounds of nasal /ŋ-/ and voiced fricative /ʒ-/.

The IAT measured the subjects' awareness towards onsets and rimes as intrasyllabic units, with the sub-tests of Onset Oddity Task (OOT) and Rime Oddity Task (ROT) designed. Both sub-tests contained 40 test items. The OOT required the subjects to identify, out of a set of four stimuli, the test word that bears an odd onset. For instance, among the prompts of *take, cake, tall,* and *talk,* the subjects must select *cake* as the odd item because it does not share the word-initial /t/, a voiceless plosive. The ROT asked the subjects to identify a test word which differed from others in terms of rime unit. For instance, among the stimulus set of *game, same, time,* and *name,* which all share the rime /em/, they had to select *time* as the odd candidate. For both sub-tests, the subjects wrote the representative number of an odd item on an answer sheet.

The SAT was adapted from the syllable doubling technique used in Fallows' (1981) study. The test contained 20 items each in Part A, which involved bisyllabic items, and Part B, which involved multisyllabic ones. The subjects had to judge accurately the structural proportions of a syllable and recognize the syllable boundary. They then had to repeat the first or last syllabic portion of a word. For example, when dealing with *a.long*, a bisyllabic stimulus, they had to follow an S1+S2→S1S1+S2 sequence (S stands for syllable), repeat the first syllable, and generate *a.a.long*. In another case of *so.fa*, they needed to follow an S1+S2→S1+S2S2 sequence, repeat the second syllable, and generate *so.fa.fa*.

Results

The subjects' performance scores on the three measures contributed to research data for quantitative analysis. Descriptive statistics were first conducted to identify their score ranges, means, and standard deviations on the measures. A one-way analysis of variance (ANOVA) was carried out to see if the subjects performed differently for different PA measures. This statistical difference revealed whether they encountered relative difficulty in processing stimuli containing phonemes (PAT), onsets and rimes (IAT), and syllables (SAT), which are phonological structures of different sizes.

	M	SD	Range
Phonemic Awareness Test (PAT)	22.73	10.45	0-61.19
Intrasyllabic Awareness Test (IAT)	42.02	10.88	0-78.75
Syllabic Awareness Test (SAT)	65.29	14.54	0-100

Table 1 Descriptive statistics of the subjects' overall performance on three PA measures (N=182)

Table 1 shows the subjects' overall performance on three PA measures. What we notice is that they performed best for the SAT, which contains stimuli involving the largest phonological structure of syllable. The mean and standard deviation are 65.29 and 14.54 respectively. For the IAT, which contains stimuli involving onsets and rimes, they performed less well. The mean and standard deviation are 42.02 and 10.88 respectively. Their scores for the PAT, which contains stimuli involving phonemes as the minimal unit, drop drastically. These scores seem to betray the effect of structural size on their phonological processing.

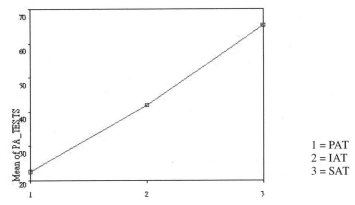

Figure 2 The mean plot of three PA measures (N = 182)

We can easily see the subjects' tendency in task performance by transforming the above descriptive statistics into a schematic presentation, like the mean plot in Figure 2. The plot shows clearly that their performance scores improve as a result of the corresponding increase in structural size. The curve shows an enormous scale of straight-up tendency.

	Sum of square	df	Mean square	Sig.
Between groups	165339.28	2	565.12***	.000
Within groups	79434.29	543		
Total	244773.5	545		

note = ***p <.001

Table 2 One-way ANOVA of means for three PA measures (N = 182)

Despite the seeming difference in the subjects' relative difficulty to cope with stimuli at different structural levels, we are a step short from judging the statistical difference in their average scores. A one-way ANOVA was carried out to this end and the outcome is displayed in Table 2. It shows a significant difference among the subjects' performance on three PA measures, $F_{(2, 543)}$ = 565.12, $p < .001$. The F value confirms the relative difficulty in processing PA measures that involve structures of different sizes: phonemes, onset and rimes, and syllables, in ascending order. The study demonstrated that the subjects' difficulty in performing PA measures decreased the same time that the structural sizes of target stimuli became larger.

Conclusion

This study explored Taiwanese children's awareness of English phonological units. Notions from the Developmental Hierarchy Hypothesis (Goswami & Bryant, 1990) were adopted to account for their development in English PA. The subjects, 182 fifth graders from a Taiwanese elementary school, took three measures that assessed their PA at phonemic, intrasyllabic, and syllabic levels. Quantitative analyses revealed that the subjects scored higher for the SAT than the IAT, which in turn out-performed the PAT. The result of ANOVA proved a significant difference in their measure means, confirming the existence of relative difficulty for English L2 children to process test stimuli of various structural sizes. Overall, the effect of structural size on Chinese-speaking children' phonological processing is thus confirmed.

Findings of the present study are in conformity with previous investigations which target English L1 learners as the subjects (Liberman, et al., 1974; Tunmer & Rohl, 1991). What those investigations agree upon is the comparative easiness for the subjects to perceive and process English syllables. This process is in a sharp contrast to the challenge that learners encounter in tackling phonemes. The difficulty to perceive and process onsets and rimes lies somewhere between these two. The issue of relative difficulty is likewise indicated in Treiman and Zukowski (1991). They find that their pre-school children perform well on the syllable task, worse on the onset-rime task, and poorly on the phoneme task. For the last one, only 25 per cent of the subjects can achieve six consecutive correct responses.

The present research also echoes opinions presented in a series of studies by Hu (1999; 2003). Hu (1999) remarkably examines the development of implicit versus explicit phonological representations among Chinese-speaking children. One of her experiments is carried out with 57 first graders in Taipei, who take the tasks of phonological memory, phonological awareness, and (Chinese) alphabetic word reading. Another experiment is done with 58 pre-schoolers in Taipei City and Taoyuan County, who take the same measures as the first grader group does. The result reveals that Chinese-speaking children's implicit phonological representations are further decomposed into more discrete subsyllabic units in the first grade.

While we feel excited about what we have achieved, we are aware of the limited generalizability that the research may produce. The applicability of our findings into other English L2 samples remains uncertain, owning to constraints concerning subject selection, sample size, and the school district from which the subjects were drawn. The subjects' entry level in English proficiency is of course a big concern as well. Despite of these limitations, we are willing to temporarily recognize the DHH as a model that explains efficiently the ways our Chinese-speaking subjects engaged in phonological processing. Hopefully, empirical inquiries with subjects from other L1 backgrounds – in particular those of non-alphabetic languages – will work to expand the generalizability of the DHH. Other than this, future researchers may want to include subjects of older ages for investigations. This inclusion is based on the recognition that the ability to analyze sounds into syllables, onset-rimes, and phonemes does increase with age (Treiman & Zukowski, 1991).

A limitation like this reminds us of the importance to seek cross-linguistic views on English L2 learners' phonological acquisition of the target language. As we may notice, child phonology has been one of the most vigorous fields in the recent two decades and it will probably remain to be so in the future. To achieve an insightful observation of the characteristics pertaining to their phonological acquisition in the TL, we need to draw on theories and paradigms from interlanguage phonology. Research looking into their behavior patterns is of supreme significance because of the expected revelation of the laws underlying their bilingual development. In the case of Chinese L1 children, an observation of their strengths and weakness in acquiring English phonology will generate linguistic data that are intriguing to look at. Carney (1994), for instance, underscores the errors made by Chinese speakers, which are due to interferences from the phonological or writing system of their native language. He notices that these learners display difficulty in pronouncing final consonant clusters. They may write '*the vowels produce by*' or '*…can still be perceive as…*', even when their knowledge of grammar should alert them to a further consonant /t/ or /d/, representing the suffix -*ed*. Cheng (1992), citing ideas from the dual access model, assumes that a skilled (Chinese) reader has an option of using either the visual or the phonological route. These two routes are thought to operate in parallel, forming a race that determines the occurrence of phonological mediation. According to Cheng, phonological information is neither necessary nor obligatory for lexical access in Chinese.

The observations of Cheng (1992) and Carney (1994) are compatible with that of d'Arcais (1992), who suggests the possible influence of the phonological processing in Chinese on that in English. As he puts it, word recognition in Chinese does not entail phonological intervention. Reading Chinese characters may completely bypass a stage of phonological encoding and require essentially the direct, lexical route. This is due to the reality that, in principle, Chinese characters can be read 'globally'. They are not translated into a phonological code 'one phoneme at a time' as is possible with alphabetic writing systems. Also noteworthy are the findings from an empirical study by Lin (2001). She examines the effect of number of English syllables on Chinese EFL learners' reduction strategies in pronouncing word-initial consonant clusters. It is found that, when encountering production difficulties for English consonant clusters, these learners generally adopt vowel epenthesis or consonant deletion. Taken together, the research evidence cited here cautions against the simplistic application of theoretical frameworks that mainly explain phonological development of English L1 learners.

The present study only serves as a modest proposal for investigating how Chinese-speaking individuals process English phonological structures. To advance our understanding in this area, we need to carry out empirical inquiries that involve more subjects from additional Chinese-speaking cultures or speech communities. These investigations are academically appealing because they help to judge fairly the different patterns pertinent to learners' acquisition of English phonology. They are productive in directing our attention to the relative difficulty that English L2 learners encounter in dealing with phonological units. Predictably, efforts of this kind will also shed light on the ways that non-native speakers strive to make themselves full-fledged learners of English phonology.

References

Bowey, J. A., and Francis, J. (1991) Phonological analysis as a function of age and exposure to reading instruction. *Applied Psycholinguistics* 12: 91–121.

Carney, E. (1994) *A Survey of English Spelling.* London: Routledge.

Cheng, C. M. (1992) Lexical access in Chinese: evidence from automatic activation of phonological information. In H. C. Chen and O. J. L. Tzeng (eds) *Language Processing in Chinese.* 67–91. Amsterdam, the Netherlands: Elsevier Science Publishers B.V.

d'Arcais, G. B. F. (1992) Graphemic, phonological, and semantic activation processes during the recognition of Chinese characters. In H. C. Chen and O. J. L. Tzeng (eds) *Language Processing in Chinese.* 37–66. Amsterdam, the Netherlands: Elsevier Science Publishers B.V.

Fallows, D. (1981) Experimental evidence of English syllabification and syllable structure. *Journal of Linguistics* 17(2): 309–17.

Ferreiro, E. and Teberosky, A. (1982) *Literacy Before Schooling.* New York: Heinemann.

Fox, B. and Routh, D. K. (1975) Analyzing spoken language into words, syllables and phonemes: a developmental study. *Journal of Psycholinguistic Research* 4: 331–42.

Fudge, E. C. (1969) Syllables. *Journal of Linguistics* 5: 253–86.

Goswami, U. (1993) Toward an interactive analogy model of reading development: decoding vowel graphemes in beginning reading. *Journal of Experimental Child Psychology* 56: 443–75.

Goswami, U. and Bryant, P. E. (1990) *Phonological Skills and Learning to Read*. London: Erlbaum.

Harris, J. (1994) *English Sound Structure*. Oxford and Cambridge, Mass.: Blackwell.

Ho, T. A. (1996) *Concepts and Methods in Phonology*. Taipei: Ta-an Publishers.

Hooper (1972) The syllable in phonological theory. *Language* 48: 522–40.

Hu, C. F. (1999) *Implicit versus Explicit Phonological Representations: the contribution of reading experience*. Research report submitted to the National Science Council of the Taiwan Government.

Hu, C. F. (2003) Phonological memory, phonological awareness, and foreign language word learning. *Language Learning* 53: 429–62.

Jensen, J. T. (1993) *English Phonology*. Amsterdam and Philadelphia: J. Benjamins.

Liberman, I. Y., Shankweiler, D. P., Fischer, F. W., and Carter, B. (1974) Explicit syllable and phoneme segmentation in the young child. *Journal of Experimental Child Psychology* 18: 201–12.

Lin, Y. H. (2001) Chinese EFL syllable simplification – the effect of Mandarin disyllabicity. In Applied English Department of Ming Chuan University (ed.) *Proceedings of the Eighteenth Conference on English Teaching and Learning in the Republic of China*. 174–85. Taipei: The Crane Publishing Co., Ltd.

MacKay, D. G. (1972) The structure of words and syllables: evidence from errors in speech. *Cognitive Psychology* 3: 210–27.

Nittrouer, S. and Studdert-Kennedy, M. (1987) The role of coarticulartory effects in the perception of fricatives by children and adults. *Journal of Speech and Hearing Research* 30: 319–29.

Nittrouer, S., Studdert-Kennedy, M. and McGowan, R. S. (1989) The emergence of phonetic segments: evidence form the spectral structure of fricative-vowel syllables spoken by children and adults. *Journal of Speech and Hearing Research* 32: 120–32.

O'Connor, J. D. and Trim, J. L. M. (1953) Vowel, consonant and syllable – a phonological definition. *Word* 9: 103–22.

Selkirk, E. (1982) The syllable. In H. Van Der Hulst and N. Smith (eds) *The Structure of Phonological Representations*. Part II. pp. 337–83. Dordrecht, The Netherlands: Foris.

Su, F. H. (2003) *The Dimensions of English Phonological Awareness*. Taipei: Win Join Book Co., Ltd.

Treiman, R. (1993) *Beginning to Spell: a study of first-grade children.* New York: Oxford University Press.

Treiman, R, and Bourassa, D. C. (2000) The development of spelling skill. *Topics in Language Disorders* 20(3): 1–18.

Treiman, R. and Chafetz, J. (1987) Are there onset- and rime-like units in printed words? In M. Coltheart (ed.) *Attention and performance XII.* 281–98. London: Erlbaum.

Treiman, R. and Zukowski, A. (1991) Levels of phonological awareness. In S. A. Brady and D. P. Shankweiler (eds) *Phonological Processes in Literacy: a tribute to Isabelle Y. Liberman.* 67–83. Hillsdale, NJ: Lawrence Erlbaum Associates.

Tunmer, W. E., and Rohl, M (1991) Phonological awareness and reading acquisition. In D. J. Sawyer and B. J. Fox (eds) *Phonological Awareness in Reading: the evolution of current perspectives.* 1–30. New York: Springer-Verlag.

Wang, J. L. and Smith, N. (1997) Introduction. In J. L. Wang and N. Smith (eds) *Studies in Chinese Phonology.* 1–12. Berlin and New York: Mouton de Gruyter.

5 Subverting conversational repair in computer-mediated communication: pseudo repair and refusal to repair in a hostile email discussion

Sandra Harrison

Coventry University

Abstract

This paper explores the use of repair-like structures in one hostile incident from a small corpus of naturally occurring email discussion data. Investigation of repair in non-hostile email discussion data revealed that a variety of patterns of repair familiar from spoken conversation were being used successfully, serving a range of purposes such as clarification of meaning, correction of factually incorrect statements, and repairs of technology-related turn-taking problems. However, it was also found that repair structures could be used for purposes other than repair, particularly in hostile episodes. This paper examines such features in one 'flaming' sequence. Here participants are found to make apparent repairs or repair initiations, which, in the context, are clearly not genuine but rather are being used to support the conflict. Similarly, participants employ repair initiators which in a genuine repair situation would be taken up by the participant in whose turn the trouble occurred, but in this context are ignored or even generate a response in the form of an overt refusal to repair. Apparent requests for clarification, seeming attempts to repair turn-taking errors, and pseudo-self-repairs are all used to add fuel to the hostilities.

Introduction

This paper investigates a hostile incident which arises on an email discussion list, and finds structures which resemble conversational repair but appear to be used in support of the hostilities rather than to resolve interactional problems. This work is part of a project which takes as its starting point the many references to electronic interaction as a form of 'conversation' (see e.g. Yates &

Orlikowski, 1993: 7, Selfe & Meyer, 1991: 188, Spinuzzi, 1994: 213). This project has used Conversation Analysis (CA) to investigate aspects of interaction in email discussions, including 'conversational' repair.

This paper will describe the data and the hostile incident, outline the nature of flaming and some of the existing research in this area, give examples of genuine repair in email discussions, and then show how repair structures are subverted in the hostile incident.

Throughout this paper, and in many of the publications cited, the term Computer Mediated Communication (CMC) is used to mean communication that takes place through the medium of computers.

The data and the hostile incident

The email discussions used in this study are naturally occurring data from UK-based email discussion lists all archived and publicly available on the JISCmail web site at http://www.jiscmail.ac.uk. For the study, 360 email messages were collected: 60 messages from each of six different email discussion lists. Samples of 60 messages were chosen because it was found that this was sufficient to allow at least one (and normally more than one) entire discussion to start, develop, and reach completion in each sample.

All of the lists in the study have a specified academic or professional focus. All are open lists (anyone can join), participation is voluntary, and the lists are unmoderated (i.e. all messages sent to the list are automatically sent to the other participants, without being filtered or edited by anyone). The samples were not selected for content except that each sample had to contain at least one complete discussion.

An initial examination of the data showed that most of the time these discussions were working well, in that if someone asked for information or raised a point for discussion they usually got a response, and the tone of most discussions was friendly. But one discussion was different. This was on a Business Ethics theme, and it begins conventionally enough with a request for information from participant A:

```
Dear Friends --

I'm preparing to teach a graduate level course in
International Business Ethics and I'm wondering
what suggestions you might have for texts or other
resources ... [the writer mentions some texts that
he has used, but adds that he is] interested in
alternative materials.
```

To this participant B responds:

> My site has lots of Web resources about corporate
> power and business ethics (or the lack thereof)--
> not as good as a formal text, but an interesting
> alternate resource. It's at [website address].
> Also, the best site out there, I think, is from
> an organization called Corporate Watch, who are at
> [website address]

At this point, participant C comes into the discussion:

> Dear B, A and others--
>
> With all due respect about your intentions, B, your
> website mentioned below reads like a compendium
> of some of the worst cliches of the myths of the
> 'socially responsible' business fiasco. It seems you
> have a difficult time distinguishing between social
> MARKETING and corporate social responsibility. I
> would hope that this list is more sophisticated than
> just a place for New Age corporate bashing. Frankly,
> the two citations you give are of that genre.
>
> I am a journalist -- I've written extensively in
> the popular press and academic journals on business
> ethics and have a column on business ethics with
> regional business publications...
>
> In fact, I am giving a key note presentation on
> the confusion of 'good intentions' with 'corporate
> responsibility' at the August International
> Association of Management Conference...
>
> In particular, my 1994 expose of Body Shop
> International -- truly one of the most dishonest
> companies I have come across in 25 years of
> journalism -- was awarded a National Press Club Award
> and has become standard teaching fare in business
> schools around the world...

[he goes on ...]

At the end of this message, which is already many times longer than the two previous messages, C adds a very long list of his own publications.

This discussion thread continues for 36 messages in total, the second longest thread in the data (the longest has 40 messages), and most of these messages are very long and hostile. A new participant, D, joins the discussion in support of C, and there follows an extended hostile interchange mostly between B, C and D.

Flaming

Flaming has been a focus of research since the earliest days of CMC. There have been various definitions of flaming, for example 'the use of invective and/or verbal aggressiveness in computer-mediated communication' Vrooman (2002: 52); 'aggressive or hostile communication occurring via computer-mediated channels' O'Sullivan and Flanigan (2003: 70); 'antisocial interaction' (Thompsen, 1996); 'hostile verbal behaviour' (Thompsen and Foulger, 1996); 'nonconforming behaviour' (Parks & Floyd, 1996); 'emotional outbursts' (Korenman & Wyatt, 1996).

Some of the earliest work on CMC focused on the absence of social cues in this medium. Often, users of CMC know nothing about the status, age, gender, race, etc., of other participants, or their reactions to what has been written, except in so far as this is revealed in the text itself. A seminal paper by Kiesler, Siegel and McGuire (1984) discussing the lack of social and paralinguistic cues in CMC concluded that this results in an absence of behavioural norms which is likely to lead to unrestrained behaviour and hence to the phenomenon of electronic abuse. This research is often quoted in later papers, but it was based on experimental studies rather than naturally occurring data, and the results have been challenged on various grounds (see e.g. Walther, 1992).

The original social cues work linked flaming behaviour only with CMC, suggesting some form of media determinism. Recent work however, has begun to look at flaming within the context of non-electronic forms of abuse. One example of this is Vrooman (2002: 53) who notes that women online are particularly subject to flaming and points out that 'Invective has traditionally been used as method of harassing women at *least* as far back as pre-Reformation England' (italics in original). Vrooman referring to work by Plotz and Bell (1996) sees flaming as a 'performance' (2002: 53) which is part of 'the creation, maintenance, and performance of identity' (2002: 53). Vrooman reasons that 'flaming as a performance would have much in common with other types of invective performance offline, performances which are also involved in this game of identity' (2002: 53). He locates flaming in the rhetorical traditions of rants and dozens, the rant being a solo criticising of society by which the ranter gains identity, especially if rejected by society, while dozens is an insult game with short turns providing social identity through the interaction and 'verbal power' (2002: 57).

Recent work has also begun to problematise the earlier assumption that it is a straightforward matter to identify flaming, questioning whether we can assume that the researcher's interpretation is the same as the writer's or other participants' interpretation. For example, O'Sullivan and Flanagin argue that one should take into account the sender's intention, the receiver's interpretation and the researcher's interpretation in a definition of flaming. They note (2003: 73) that the 'the casual use of profane language among close friends can be a marker of relationship closeness', and that other instances of apparent hostility could in fact arise from miscommunication. They believe that the sender's intention has to be taken into account in order to determine whether what occurs is a flame (deliberate hostility) or a miscommunication (unintentionally coming over as hostile). McKee (2002) takes a similar position on this, and problematises the concept of flame in a cross-cultural context, showing that messages are interpreted very differently by different readers and by the sender: one reader will interpret as a deliberate flame, what a different reader, or the sender, may interpret as not a flame.

However, it is not always possible to question message senders about their communicative intentions or recipients about their interpretations. Where the entire communication is taking place electronically (as in my own data) the researcher's access to the text is the same as the participants', but even in this situation the researcher's interpretation could still differ from that of the participants. I address this problem by looking for evidence from within the text itself to determine whether the apparently hostile incident should indeed be interpreted as a flame (see below).

Evidence of flaming

In fact, there is evidence throughout the Business Ethics thread that this is a hostile and abusive sequence:

1. There is unmitigated disagreement. Pomerantz (1984) has shown that in conversation disagreement is a non-preferred response and is therefore usually mitigated in some way. Several subsequent studies on different types of data have supported this finding: for example Lockyer and Pickering's (2001: 640) work on complaint letters to *Private Eye*, Mulkay's (1985) work on agreements and disagreements in letters written by biochemists, and my own work on politeness strategies in email discussions (Harrison, 2000), all find that disagreements typically begin with a positive expression or an agreement, or some other preface in explanation or justification or mitigation of the disagreement. C's first message, quoted above, has a minimal preface and makes a long unmitigated attack on B, thus breaking with our expectations of mitigated disagreement.

2. C's first message also breaks a convention that is found in my email data: C ends this message with a very long list of his own publications. The unsolicited sending of a personal publication list is not found anywhere else in the data. Bibliographies may be offered on email discussion lists but are usually provided off list. Occasionally a bibliography will be requested, and in this case it may be sent over the list. But nowhere else in the data is a bibliography sent over the list without being requested. Moreover, in this particular case the items in the bibliography are all the sender's own work, and the bibliography is therefore clearly serving the function of emphasising his own merits. This may be contrasted with B's offer of his own website in the second message in this thread, which is more typical of the way in which participants refer to their own works. B offers his website in direct response to a request for information, presenting it as a gateway to 'lots of Web resources' (which are not his own work). B even downplays his site by describing it as 'not as good as a formal text', and by providing additionally the address of the Corporate Watch website which he describes as 'the best site out there'.

3. Conversation analysis prompts us to see how the listener orients to what is said. In C's first message, he is addressing B. When we look at B's reaction to this message, we find that he describes it as:

    ```
    your vitriolic response to my simple offer of help
    ```

    and throughout this discussion thread B repeatedly uses similar terms to describe messages from C. Indeed, some of the words used by the participants in the hostile incident to describe each others' messages echo the definitions of flaming cited in the 'Flaming' section above.

4. There is evidence from two participants not involved in the flame. This is a long thread with very few participants, but two non-combatants do make contributions. The first of these refers to 'personal vituperation', 'expletives', 'smallmindedness and pique' – all indicators of flaming – and asks for a more reasonable approach. The second non-combatant is so annoyed by the hostilities that they have decided to leave the list. This is a tactic similar to walking away from a face-to-face discussion, except that simply leaving the list would not be visible to the other participants, so this participant has chosen to send an exit message to explain their reason for leaving:

    ```
    When I first subscribed to this list, I did so with
    the impression that I would be learning something
    about business and ethics and the like. Instead, this
    seems to be a list for immature, vitriolic, sarcastic
    diatribes and snipes ...
    ```

```
I, for one, have no desire to be a party to the on-
going useless debate. I therefore wish to UNSUBSCRIBE
from this list. Thank you.
```

There is therefore considerable evidence within the data to show that participants are not treating this as an acceptable discussion.

Repair

Conversation is generally unplanned, and is produced and managed in real time, with the result that it is subject to innumerable minor problems, as discussed widely in CA (see e.g. Sacks et al., 1974). Hutchby and Wooffitt define repair:

> This is a generic term which is used in CA to cover a wide range of phenomena, from seeming errors in turn-taking such as those involved in much overlapping talk, to any of the forms of what we commonly would call 'correction' – that is, substantive faults in the contents of what someone has said. (1998: 57)

Indeed repair may be carried out 'even when there is no error or mistake in the conversation' (Hutchby & Wooffitt, 1998: 60), for example to produce a word more suited to the needs of the recipient.

Discussions about repair usually characterise the repair according to who initiates it, and who carries it out:

> The initiative can be taken by the speaker of the repairable, which is called a 'self-initiated repair', or others can take such an initiative, 'other-initiated repair'. And the repair itself can be done by the original speaker, 'self-repair', or by others, 'other repair'. (ten Have, 1999: 116)

Examples of self-initiated self-repair in conversation include self-correction in the middle of an utterance (Hutchby & Wooffitt, 1998: 61–2), or some kind of corrective action when it is clear from the listener's next turn that s/he has misunderstood (ten Have, 1999: 116).

Examples of other-initiated self-repair include use of a 'next-turn repair initiator (NTRI)' (Hutchby & Wooffitt, 1998: 62) such as 'huh?' or 'what?' (ten Have 1999: 116) which prompts the original speaker to repair. Or the next speaker may 'offer a candidate understanding of a target utterance, possibly in a format like "you mean X?"' (ten Have, 1999: 116).

Self-initiated other-repair would include situations such as the speaker attempting to remember a name and asking the listener(s) for assistance (Hutchby & Wooffit, 1998: 61).

Other-initiated other-repair 'is closest to what is conventionally understood as "correction"' (Hutchby & Wooffitt, 1998: 61).

Repair in CMC

There has been very little work on repair in CMC. Even those studies which have identified problems in the interaction have not then extended this to include a discussion of how the troubles are repaired. For example, McLaughlin *et al* (1995) list factors that generate complaints in newsgroups, including technology-related problems, breaking of established conventions, 'Inappropriate language' and 'Factual errors' (1995: 96–7), but do not link these problems to conversational repair. Cherny makes brief references to instances of repair in her MUD data, commenting on 'clarifying questions' (1995: 219), i.e. other-initiated repair, and an instance (1995: 221) of a participant explaining what is being responded to when another message intervenes to disrupt turn adjacency, i.e. self-initiated repair. However, these mentions of problems and brief references to repair-like features do not constitute an investigation into repair in CMC.

An examination of the email discussion data shows that there are indeed features that resemble repair. However, repair in email discussions differs from repair in conversation in that it clearly does not have those repairs which are the outcome of real-time spoken interaction, such as dealing with simultaneous speech and the self-repair of a term or construction mid-sentence as soon as it has been produced. These particular problems are largely absent from email discussions because the interaction takes place in writing. If participants take several attempts to produce a word, if they decide to change a word or expression, they would normally delete their earlier attempts. The written equivalent of adjustment of talk in progress is editing, but the reader has no access to either the editing process or the original text – we see only the end product, the message as it was sent, and cannot even know whether the text has been edited. So in email any observable repair is usually 'exposed' (Jefferson, 1987) and explicitly signalled by the writer or another participant. And indeed there is clear evidence of repair taking place in email discussions: self- and other-initiated self- and other-repair are found, serving a range of purposes such as clarification of meaning, correction of factually incorrect statements, and repairs of technology-related turn-taking problems.

Self-repair

Problems with turn-taking are not common in email discussions because there can be no problems of interruptions or simultaneous speech in this type of discourse (though see the 'Subverting Repair' section below for turn-taking errors which arise from participants not attending to the whole of a discussion). When turn-taking errors do occur, they may be the result of the speaker's interaction with the technology, for example the sending of 'empty' messages. In many cases, this will pass without comment, and if observed by the sender the problem will be repaired simply by sending the message again. Occasionally this will be accompanied by a comment such as the following:

```
My previous attempt having failed-I'll try again from
work
```

which makes the repair explicit.

Self-repair can also be used for clarification. In another example a sender self-repairs in order to clarify an ambiguity that he has noticed in one of his previous messages. At the start of the repair message he quotes the relevant sentence from his original message, where it is not clear whether '119' is the total sample, the number who responded, or the number of respondents who asked for feedback.

```
When I said:

"They also say in huge numbers (119 in sample) that
FEEDBACK is what they crave!"

I should clarify:

"huge" was a bit of an exaggeration (I'm excited,
can't you tell!) and 119 was the total number of
returns out of c700 questionnaires sent out - most
of these 119, however, cite feedback as a major
priority.
```

Other initiated repair and NTRIs

As Schegloff, Jefferson and Sacks (1977) have shown, there is a marked preference for self-repair. Unmitigated repair by someone other than the original speaker can be threatening to the original speaker, so if another speaker wishes to initiate a repair they typically use a prompt, described as a 'next-turn repair initiator (NTRI)' (Hutchby & Wooffitt, 1998: 62). The element that is being repaired can itself be the first or second part of an exchange pair, and it is followed by a repair pair, of the form (prompt + repair). In the data, next-turn repair initiators mostly take the form of requests for clarification or for correction, such as the conventional 'Do you mean', in the example below. The trouble source was located in an earlier message where the original sender mentioned work by 'Carol Myer'. The recipient of this original message makes a next-turn repair initiator which is a request for clarification:

```
Hey, thanks for the help. Do you mean Carol Meyers?
```

This is mitigated somewhat by the thanks at the start of the message, and receives a response from the original sender realising the repair:

```
Yes, I heard her speak a few years ago...
```

It can be seen from this example that the original speaker orients to the next-turn repair initiator as a prompt for repair, and she produces the repair in her next message.

This is normal throughout our data except in the hostile incident: next-turn repair initiators are oriented to as prompts for repair and the repair follows very closely after the prompt, often in the adjacent turn, despite the problems of 'disrupted turn *adjacency*' (Herring, 1999: 3, italics in the original) found in these asynchronous discussions.

Subverting repair

An examination of the hostile incident reveals that there are utterances which seem to have similar structures to some of the genuine repairs, but appear to be serving quite a different purpose.

Apparent requests for clarification

As outlined above, the 'genuine' instances of repair include NTRIs in the form of requests for clarification. In the hostile incident too there are features which appear to take the form of next-turn repair initiators. For example, we have an apparent request for clarification when D asks:

```
B, did I miss something?
```

A reading of the message suggests that this is ironic and not a request for clarification, and this impression is confirmed by B's reply. Although B responds in the adjacent message he does not carry out a repair, suggesting that he too did not interpret this as a genuine next-turn repair initiator requesting clarification.

In another message the participant begins with 'Huh?' – a prototypical form of next-turn repair initiator as in the example from ten Have (1999: 116) above:

```
Huh? C makes a comment worthy of a 13-year old
and I'm to feel shame? And this from somebody who
collects far more tax money (as a professor and a
businessman) than I do? Please help me to understand.
```

We have here a pair of apparent next-turn repair initiators, 'Huh?' and 'Please help me to understand', but here too the rest of the message suggests that this is not a genuine request for clarification, and in fact C does not orient to it as a next-turn repair initiator – it receives no repair and indeed no response at all.

Pseudo-self-repairs

There are also apparent self-initiated self-repairs where the original speaker says the second speaker has misinterpreted something which the original speaker then appears to clarify. Thus in the first hostile message C gave an assessment of B's website:

> ```
> With all due respect about your intentions, B, your
> website mentioned below reads like a compendium
> of some of the worst cliches of the myths of the
> 'socially responsible' business fiasco. It seems you
> have a difficult time distinguishing between social
> MARKETING and corporate social responsibility.
> ```
>
> ```
> I would hope that this list is more sophisticated
> than just a place for New Age corporate bashing.
> Frankly, the two citations you give are of that
> genre...
> ```

In his next message, B refers to this as a "vitriolic response", but C treats this as a misinterpretation, and carries out an apparent self-initiated self-repair in his next turn:

> ```
> That's funny. My words were rather measured...
> ```

However, C's first message was clearly rather 'vitriolic', so C is doing something other than repair here – perhaps suggesting that in fact he was being more restrained than he might have been, and thereby emphasising his attack.

Later in the thread, E comes into the fray with comments such as:

> ```
> I have been following B's rather inconsiderate and
> intemperate exchange with C and D, and had decided
> that there was more emotion than fact in B's posts...
> ```
>
> ```
> It is sad that some academics have bought into the
> shallow and largely unfounded perspective that B
> and other business-bashers continue to broadcast to
> anyone who is niave [sic] enough to listen...
> ```

Here we have several words which attack B who then describes the content of E's message as 'emotional attacks', but E frames this as a misunderstanding and appears to give a clarification of his original message:

```
B, if I were to attack you "emotionally" I would
certainly use words other than "inconsiderate" and
"intemperate."
```

However, E does use 'other' words, including 'business-bashers', which could very well be considered to be 'emotional'.

Seeming attempts to repair turn-taking errors

We can also observe some seeming attempts to repair turn-taking errors. Although participants in email discussions do not have to deal with the problem of overlapping turns, a potential turn-taking problem in email discussions is that participants may not have been following a particular thread, or may have skipped part of the exchange. Because of the different turn-taking rules in email discussions, it is not necessary for each participant to attend to every turn (as it is in conversation). However, when a participant decides to contribute to a discussion which they have not been following, there is a potential for errors such as repeating what has already been said, or making an off-topic contribution. Here is a genuine instance from elsewhere in the data where a participant is aware of this danger and prefaces her contribution with an apology:

```
I haven't been following this thread so I may be
coming in from the wrong angle and repeating things
that have already been said - sorry.
```

In the hostile incident, participants suggest that similar turn-taking problems have occurred: on several occasions a participant suggests that another participant has not been reading the contributions, for example from B:

```
Jeez Professor, at least I can be reasonably sure
that C actually READS my posts! Why not take a look
through them again and reconsider your emotional
attacks....
```

Similarly, a few messages later, D writes:

```
B, read the rest of that message.
```

These are apparently next-turn repair initiators prompting the other speaker to repair a turn-taking error and attend to the content of previous turns. However, in the context of flaming they do not seem to be genuine next-turn repair initiators, and this is confirmed by the fact that no repair actually takes place.

Refusal to repair

Finally, it is possible for a speaker to refuse next-turn repair initiators or other-repair, although no studies have been found which discuss this. In conversation this can occur in contexts which are not hostile, for example, it could take the form of the second speaker questioning the first speaker's word or usage and the first speaker affirming that their choice was correct. There are refusals to repair in the Business Ethics flaming sequence, for example, we find a next-turn repair initiator prompting a repair to the tone of the discussion:

        Let's get beyond the cheap sarcasm, OK?

This is followed by a response which is a refusal to repair:

        There is nothing cheap about my sarcasm.

Conclusion

In conclusion, we can find evidence in the text of the Business Ethics email discussion to support the interpretation that this is a hostile incident. This is important in the current context of research into flaming because of the problematisation of the identification of flaming.

Then, by looking at genuine instances of repair in email discussions and comparing these with the hostile discussion, we can observe structures resembling repair that have been subverted for hostile use. This interpretation is supported by the participants' own orientation to the interaction.

This is not to suggest that such subversion of repair is unique to flaming in CMC. Indeed, it is likely that it also occurs when hostile episodes arise in spoken conversation, but no papers have been found that discuss this. The results of this study therefore suggest interesting avenues for further exploration both in electronic and face-to-face contexts.

Note

1. The ethical issues raised by the use of naturally occurring email data have been addressed in this study as follows. This work uses only data which are in the public domain. The data are taken from open discussion lists which are archived on a web site to which access is not restricted, and participants are advised upon joining these email lists that their discussions will be archived in this way. In addition, participant names have been anonymised and any participant contact details removed.

References

Cherny, L. (1995) The MUD register: conversational modes of action in a text-based virtual reality. PhD thesis, Stanford University. Available from http://www.research .att.com/~cherny/chap1.ps Accessed 10/7/1998.

Harrison, S. (2000) Maintaining the virtual community: use of politeness strategies in an email discussion group. In L. Pemberton and S. Shurville (eds) *Words on the Web: computer mediated communication*. 69–78. Exeter: Intellect.

Have, P. ten (1999) *Doing Conversation Analysis: a practical guide*. London: Sage.

Herring, S. (1999) Interactional Coherence in CMC. *Journal of Computer-Mediated Communication* 4: 4. http://www.ascusc.org/jcmc/vol4/issue4/herring.html Accessed 18/12/2001.

Hutchby, I. and Wooffitt, R. (1998) *Conversation Analysis: principles, practices and applications*. Cambridge: Polity Press.

Jefferson, G. (1987) On exposed and embedded correction in conversation. In G. Button and J. Lee (eds) *Talk and Social Organisation*. 86–100. Clevedon England: Multilingual Matters.

Kiesler, S., Siegel, J. and McGuire, T. (1984) Social psychological aspects of computer mediated communication. *American Psychologist* 39(10): 1123–34.

Korenman, J. and Wyatt, N. (1996) Group Dynamics in an E-Mail Forum. In S. Herring (ed.) *Computer-Mediated Communication: linguistic, social and cross-cultural perspectives*. 225–42. Amsterdam: John Benjamins.

Lockyer, S. and Pickering, M. (2001) 'Dear shit-shovellers: humour, censure and the discourse of complaint.' *Discourse and Society* 12(5): 633–51.

McKee, H. (2002) "YOUR VIEWS SHOWED TRUE IGNORANCE!!!": (Mis)Communication in an online interracial discussion forum. *Computers and Composition* 19: 411–34.

McLaughlin, M., Osborne, K. and Smith, C. (1995) Standards of Conduct on Usenet. In S. Jones (ed.) *CyberSociety: computer mediated communication and community*. 90–111. Thousand Oaks, California: Sage.

Mulkay, M. (1985) Agreement and disagreement in conversation and letters. *Text* 5(3): 201–27.

O'Sullivan, P. and Flanigan, A. (2003) Reconceptualizing 'flaming' and other problematic messages. *New Media and Society* 5(1): 69–94.

Parks, M. and Floyd, K. (1996) Making Friends in Cyberspace. *Journal of Communication* 46(1): 80–97.

Plotz, T. and Bell, E. (1996) Invisible Rendezvous: mapping the music and community of computer mediated communication through performance (point and counterpoint). *Text and Performance Quarterly* 16,1: 172–88.

Pomerantz, A. (1984) Agreeing and disagreeing with assessments: some features of preferred/dispreferred turn shapes. In J. Atkinson and J. Heritage (eds) *Structures of Social Action: studies in conversation analysis.* 57–101. Cambridge: Cambridge University Press.

Sacks, H., Schegloff, E. and Jefferson, G. (1974) A simplest systematics for the organization of turn-taking for conversation. *Language* 50: 696–735.

Schegloff, E., Jefferson, G. and Sacks, H. (1977) The preference for self-correction in the organisation of repair in conversation. *Language* 53: 361–82.

Selfe, C. and Meyer, P. (1991) Testing claims for on-line conferences. *Written Communication* 8(2): 163–92.

Spinuzzi, C. (1994) A different kind of forum: rethinking rhetorical strategies for electronic text media. *IEEE Transactions on Professional Communication* 37(4): 213–17.

Thompsen, P. (1996) What's fuelling the flames in cyberspace? A social influence model. In L. Strate, R. Jacobsen and S. Gibson (eds) *Communication and Cyberspace: social interaction in an electronic environment.* 297–315. Cresskill, NJ: Hampton Press.

Thompsen, P. and Foulger D. (1996) Effects of pictographs and quoting in electronic mail. *Computers in Human Behavior* 12(2): 225–43.

Vrooman, S. (2002) The art of invective: performing identity in cyberspace. *New Media and Society* 4(1): 51–70.

Walther, J. (1992) Interpersonal effects in computer-mediated interaction. *Communication Research* 19(1): 52–90.

Yates, J. and Orlikowski, W. (1993) *Knee-Jerk Anti-LOOPism and other E-mail Phenomena: oral, written, and electronic patterns in computer mediated communication.* Cambridge Mass: Massachusetts Institute of Technology, Working Paper WP#3578–93 June 1993.

6 Citation analysis: a multidisciplinary perspective on academic literacy

Nigel Harwood

University of Essex

Abstract

The acquisition of academic literacy for students of English is problematic. One of the reasons for this is that academic writing is, in Theresa Lillis' (1999) words, 'an institutional practice of mystery', poorly understood by students and lecturers alike. The act of citation is particularly underexplored by researchers and practitioners of English for Academic Purposes (EAP). Work on explaining the phenomena of citation and attribution in academic texts has been carried out in three fields, Information Science, Sociology of Science, and Applied Linguistics. While an applied linguistics perspective highlights similarities and differences between the writer's use of direct/indirect and integral/non-integral quotations, this paper focuses on the Information Science and Sociology of Science literature which is perhaps less well known to TESOL theorists and practitioners. Information scientists and sociologists show how citation can be viewed from either a normative or social constructionist perspective. The normative model sees acknowledging others as an act of dispensing credit, putting on record the debt the writer owes their colleagues for borrowing ideas or results. In contrast, the social constructionist model claims that citing helps the writer make their paper more persuasive. I explore these two perspectives by qualitatively analyzing a corpus of Physics articles, and argue that the writers' citations can be interpreted according to the normative or social constructionist models. In fact the citations can be seen to fulfill both functions simultaneously, as they help the writer create a research space, foreground the novelty and methodological soundness of analysis, and confer disciplinary legitimacy upon the writer by linking them with well-established figures in their field. The paper ends by arguing that a corpus-based approach to citation analysis will help EAP teachers promote a type of academic literacy which inducts learners into some of the social practices which are part of the act of academic writing itself.

Introduction

Traditionally, literacy has been seen as static, unified, and easily described and understood. Indeed, many lecturers consciously or unconsciously continue to take this view, believing 'that at some point in their lives, students can attain a unitary macroskill that will enable them to move immediately from an illiterate to a literate state' (Johns, 1997: 72–3). However, researchers now stress how literacy is situated and socially constructed. It is more accurate to talk of literacies than literacy, since '[l]iteracy is embedded in institutional contexts that shape the practices and social meanings attached to reading and writing' (Barton, 1991: 10). In other words, different literacies are appropriate in different contexts; and in an academic context, an appropriate literacy will not be achieved merely by having a command of a range of grammatical and lexical features. Learners must also demystify the practices of academic writing, asking why particular language appears in particular texts, and investigating 'what personal or social factors influence linguistic choices' (Johns, 1997: 6). Here I argue that although most English for Academic Purposes (EAP) practitioners and materials writers treat the act of citing as just another grammatical or lexical feature, by drawing upon the research on citation analysis in the disciplines of Information Science and Sociology of Science, EAP teachers can begin to give their students an insight into the social and institutional factors which shape academic writing.

I begin by claiming that academic writing practices often remain obscure to EAP students. I then describe two theories of the act of citation found in the Information Science and Sociology of Science literature, before illustrating these theories by drawing upon a small corpus of Physics articles. The multifunctional view of citation that emerges is contrasted with the simplistic coverage of citation in EAP textbooks, and I conclude by arguing that materials designers would be enhancing postgraduate students' academic literacy if they drew attention to these functions.

Academic writing as an institutional practice of mystery

As Theresa Lillis (1999) has argued, academic writing practices are poorly understood by both teachers and students. Lillis' assertion is supported by research taking place in a number of areas. Corpus studies and ethnographies, for instance, have demonstrated that academic discourse varies enormously from field to field, consisting of a mass of disciplinary and sub-disciplinary variations (e.g. Hyland, 2000; 2002; Prior, 1998). Qualitative interviews with students reveal that although some faculty continue to believe that academic discourse is a homogeneous, easily identifiable phenomenon which can be taught unproblematically by EAP support units, students are presented with a different understanding of what precisely constitutes 'good writing' depending on which lecturers they talk to (Lea & Stierer, 2000). Students are obliged to change their writing style from assignment to assignment in an attempt to give the lecturer the kind of writing they require (Lea & Street, 2000). Finally, students' own retrospective accounts of how they came to terms with life in the academy (e.g. Fan Shen, 1989; Fox, 1994) reveal the formidable nature of the challenge to produce successful writing. While the acquisition of academic literacy may be akin to a game (Casanave, 2002; Newman, 2001), it is a game with a bewildering set of rules, many of which are never made explicit to student writers. Unfortunately, as far as citation is concerned, many EAP textbooks do very little to demystify these rules, as we shall see. However, I first outline the two main theories of citation, before illustrating these with corpus extracts.

A multidisciplinary view of citation

The normative/reward view

The traditional view of citations from the Information Science perspective is that they acknowledge researchers' property rights. According to Kaplan (1965), a tension exists at the heart of scholarly endeavour due to the scientist's desire to communicate their discoveries on the one hand, while preventing their claims from being stolen by their peers on the other. This tension is resolved by citation: while the entire academic community 'own' ideas, researchers have a duty to acknowledge intellectual indebtedness, using the citation to reward the discoverer with credit. Recognition, then, is dispensed strictly according to merit (i.e. the originality and worth of ideas and findings). Thus citation is above all an ethical practice.

The rhetorical/social constructionist view

Citation and persuasion

Advocates of the rhetorical view argue that the normative communistic view of the academy is stylized and naïve, bearing no resemblance to the reality in which peers struggle for recognition and promotion. Since it is one's peers who have the power to cite or ignore a claim, the more convincing one's research, the more likely it is to be quoted. So citations are used to increase the rhetoricity of a text, in the hope that the work will be cited in turn by the community. Hence the overarching purpose of citation is persuasion (Brooks, 1985; 1986; Gilbert, 1977; Latour & Woolgar, 1979).

A rhetorical citation taxonomy

Moravcsik and Murugesan's (1975) groundbreaking study was the first to posit a largely rhetorical citation taxonomy. They argued that not all citations were necessary. While *organic* references are references which are genuinely needed by the citer to enable their paper to be understood, *perfunctory* references are 'mainly an acknowledgement that some other work in the same general area has been performed', thus being to some extent decorative (Moravcsik & Murugesan, 1975: 88), trophies from one's reading (White, 2001: 104). Expanding on the concept of the perfunctory reference, Moravcsik and Murugesan (1975: 90) refer to what they term 'redundant' citations, 'when a reference is made to several papers, each of which makes the same point'. Their explanation for the existence of redundant citations is as follows:

> In such cases from a strictly scientific point of view, reference to one single paper would be sufficient, and the multiple reference is made mainly to 'keep everybody happy' in the game of priority hunting. (Moravcsik & Murugesan, 1975: 90)

and they report that about a third of the citations from their study fell into this category. In some ways, then, Moravcsik and Murugesan's choice of terminology is unfortunate. While such citations may be 'redundant' in terms of making the text comprehensible, they clearly perform an important rhetorical function.

Citations can also be omitted: a writer may decide to cite only one or two representative sources for reasons of parsimony (MacRoberts & MacRoberts, 1986; 1996; Vinkler, 1987). A desire for stylistic elegance and succinctness undoubtedly provides a partial explanation for this (Whitley, 2000), as does the space restrictions placed upon writers by journals, and the finite time and patience of the readership. However, there are two other reasons for parsimony, both of which fit in well with the rhetorical view of citation. Firstly, selective citing is the cause of the so-called 'Matthew Effect' (Merton, 1968), which posits that researchers with high profiles will be the ones who will tend to be cited, while their less well-known counterparts will often fail to attract citations even if they produce papers of a similar quality. This is because it is more rhetorically effective to cite a selection of papers which the audience will view as important, authored by big hitters. Indeed, Gilbert (1977) goes as far as to argue that rhetorical concerns may override issues of relevance: 'respected papers may be cited in order to shine in their reflected glory even if they do not seem closely related to the substantive content [of the paper being written]' (p.116). Secondly, by choosing to cite one paper over another which would equally serve their purposes, the researcher is effectively displaying their allegiance to a particular ideological camp (Gilbert, 1977), prolonging the life and influence of the cited author's claim. The payback is, of course, that the writer hopes to be cited by the others in their camp in turn, which will also prolong the life of their own work.

Having outlined the normative and rhetorical theories, I now draw upon extracts from my corpus which feature citation, and identify three distinct effects the citations help to achieve. I argue that most of these citations can be interpreted in line with either the normative or the rhetorical perspective. It should be noted that, because the physicists use the footnote referencing system, citations in the extracts appear in the form of a superscript number (e.g. [3]).

Corpus analysis
Building on others' work

Citations allow the writer to display their reliance on others' work. In the extract below, the writers name those responsible for the work they are dependent upon, despite being under no obligation to do so, given physicists' use of the footnote system of referencing:

> Figure 4(a) illustrates the model used. The ground and excited state potential energy surfaces (PES) are from ab initio calculations of Avouris et al. on hydrogenated silicon clusters [28]. (Phys 4)

A normative take on this would claim that the writers name the researchers to underscore their debt of gratitude. A rhetorical/social constructionist take, on the other hand, would argue that the citation is pressganged into service by the writers to enhance the persuasiveness of their research. This earlier work has already been ratified by the community's gatekeepers as 'valid science' (Gilbert, 1977). The writer will therefore strengthen their claim to be producing high quality research by associating themselves with this knowledge. This association will also diminish the chances of a critical response to the writer's work, since the critic would need to weaken the cited papers' claims as well as the claims of the text which cites them (Latour, 1987; Small, 1998). Alternatively, perhaps the researcher named in the extract is a big hitter in the discipline; or perhaps their research has been especially influential. The association with such research can only be to the writer's advantage.

A normative interpretation of the next extract would see the citation as triggered by the writers' debt to others:

> We have taken into account the fact that the Si(l00)-(2 X 1):H surface possesses C2 symmetry with two equally populated domains orthogonal to each other [20]. (Phys 4)

Had the cited researchers' work not been taken into account, the writers' findings may have been methodologically suspect. A rhetorical interpretation of the extract, however, would argue that the citation helps the writers to construct themselves as scientists of integrity and masters of their discipline. By demonstrating to the audience how much care they have taken to get their methodology right, the researchers are enhancing the persuasiveness of their work.

Novelty/advancing disciplinary knowledge

The examples analyzed in this section occur at the beginning of the Physics papers. The researcher in the first extract is honest enough to acknowledge that they are not alone in proposing solutions to a problem:

> We concentrate on this particular scenario, but note that there are other interesting suggestions [4] for a low effective Planck or string scale.
> (Phys 1)

According to a normative perspective, then, the writer is ensuring that the credit for innovative research is distributed fairly. Indeed, not only does the writer recognize their peers' contribution to knowledge, they also look favourably upon it, describing it as *interesting*, an adjective which signifies positive evaluation (Hunston, 1989; Thompson & Hunston, 2000). A rhetorical interpretation, however, would point out that the writers have also subtly evaluated their own work as *interesting*, along with the cited research. They are creating a research space, and underscoring the novelty of their own contribution to knowledge.

The next extract is similar:

> The usefulness of the SQUID magnetometer…is well known [1]. (Phys 2)

The writers foreground the value of their findings by using the positively evaluative *usefulness*, bolstering the credibility of their evaluation by means of a citation, which shows that their opinion is shared by others in the community. Coming at the start of the paper, this judgement is designed to demonstrate to the readership that the writers' research is newsworthy.

Self-promotion (and self-citation)

Writers cite themselves when they use the same methodology or calculations they used in earlier work:

> To demonstrate the superconductivity-induced suppression of GMR, we use the method outlined in [11] to compute the zero-bias, zero-temperature conductance of the (Cu/Co)nPb multilayer sketched in Fig. 1…. (Phys 3)

A normative interpretation would presumably stress the importance of acknowledging debts, even if those debts are to oneself. However, a rhetorical perspective reveals the subtle self-promotional tenor the writers are introducing into their texts in examples such as these. The writers construct themselves as rigorous researchers by relying on previous work which the community has accepted as valid – but the fact that the work in question is their own helps them present themselves as serious players in their discipline (Bonzi & Snyder, 1991).

Writers can also use self-citations to avoid giving exhaustive accounts of procedures and/or results in the paper they are composing:

> High-quality spectra of 25 quasars were obtained, in which intervening absorption systems at low/intermediate redshift have been identified exhibiting Fe II, Mg II, and other species. Full observational details are given in Ref. [3]. (Phys 5)

> We describe the details of the theoretical developments in a separate paper, [4] here summarizing the main points. (Phys 5)

While such self-citations can be attributed to a desire to save space, given the severe restrictions on length imposed on the Physics letter, a rhetorical reading would put such instances of self-citation down to a desire to ensure the readership is aware of the writers' other work.

This brief analysis has hopefully demonstrated that citation can be viewed as a multifunctional pragmatic act. Its complexity is now contrasted with the simplistic view of citation put forward in many EAP textbooks.

EAP textbooks' view of citation

Thompson (2001) analyzed how five of the most popular EAP textbooks teach citation, and found their treatment was less than satisfactory. For instance, Jordan (1990) is said to concentrate on 'the form of the citation rather than the purpose' (Thompson, 2001: 197), while Trzeciak and MacKay (1994) offer 'little in the way of clear guidance to the apprentice writer and no discussion of disciplinary differences' (Thompson, 2001: 198). And although two of the textbooks (Swales & Feak (1994) and Weissberg & Buker (1990)) are praised for their more comprehensive treatment, materials writers generally focus on 'a small set of mechanical features associated with citation' (Thompson & Tribble, 2001: 100), at the expense of more fundamental issues. This assertion is supported by Borg (2000: 28), who complains that 'there is little discussion of why students and academic authors should or do cite others and little thoughtful guidance on why this is necessary'. Rather than drawing on the normative and rhetorical perspectives to try to raise learners' awareness of the functions of citation, then, many EAP textbooks go no further than explaining the similarities and differences between the Footnote and Harvard systems of referencing, or, in Campbell's (1990: 226) words, reproduce 'anxiety-producing harangue[s] about plagiarism'.

While I lack the space here to replicate any full-scale analysis of textbooks' treatment of citation, I briefly review the approaches of a few other popular textbooks. In Matthews et al. (2000), for instance, there is a preoccupation with ensuring students include the correct references, and avoid misspelling the names of their sources. Huckin and Olsen (1991) are chiefly concerned with explaining the similarities and differences between the Harvard and Footnote systems. Clanchy and Ballard (1998) and Day (1998) are similar, but they also stress the importance of getting the mechanics of citation right, like quoting Internet sources correctly. Finally, although Swales and Feak's (2000) corpus-based awareness-raising approach is arguably more sophisticated than any of its rivals (Harwood, 2003), the spotlight remains on how citation is used, rather than what it is for.

Conclusion

Although most of the research into citation has been done in the Information Science/Sociology of Science arena, it is work which linguists and EAP materials writers would do well to draw upon and adapt for pedagogical purposes. Raising learners' awareness of the pragmatic purposes as well as the mechanics behind the act of citing will give the class an insight into the 'personal or social factors [which] influence linguistic choices' in the academy (Johns, 1997: 6). Students' academic literacy will be developed by concentrating on the why as well as on the how of citation.

References

Barton, D. (1991) The social nature of writing. In D. Barton and R. Ivanič (eds) *Writing in the Community*. 1–13. Newbury Park: Sage Publications.

Bonzi, S. and Snyder, H. W. (1991) Motivations for citation: a comparison of self citation and citation to others. *Scientometrics* 21(2): 245–54.

Borg, E. (2000) Citation practices in academic writing. In P. Thompson (ed.) *Patterns and Perspectives: insights into EAP writing practice*. 26–44. Reading: Centre for Applied Language Studies, University of Reading.

Brooks, T. A. (1985) Private acts and public objects: an investigation of citer motivations. *Journal of the American Society for Information Science* 36(4): 223–9.

Brooks, T. A. (1986) Evidence of complex citer motivations. *Journal of the American Society for Information Science* 37(1): 34–6.

Campbell, C. (1990) Writing with others' words: using background reading text in academic compositions. In B. Kroll (ed.) *Second Language Writing: research insights for the classroom.* 211–30. Cambridge: Cambridge University Press.

Casanave, C. P. (2002) *Writing Games: multicultural case studies of academic literacy practices in higher education.* Mahwah, NJ: Lawrence Erlbaum Associates.

Clanchy, J. and Ballard, B. (1998) *How to Write Essays: a practical guide for students* (third edition). Melbourne: Longman.

Day, R. A. (1998) *How to Write and Publish a Scientific Paper* (fifth edition). Cambridge: Cambridge University Press.

Fan Shen, (1989) The classroom and the wider culture: identity as a key to learning English composition. *College Composition and Communication* 40(4:) 459–66.

Fox, H. (1994) *Listening to the World: cultural issues in academic writing.* Urbana, Illinois: National Council of Teachers of English.

Gilbert, G. N. (1977) Referencing as persuasion. *Social Studies of Science* 7: 113–22.

Harwood, N. (2003) What do we want EAP teaching materials for? Paper presented at IATEFL, Brighton.

Huckin, T. N. and Olsen, L. A. (1991) *Technical Writing and Professional Communication for Non-native Speakers of English* (international edition) (second edition). New York: McGraw-Hill.

Hunston, S. (1989) Evaluation in experimental research articles. Unpublished PhD thesis, University of Birmingham.

Hyland, K. (2000) *Disciplinary Discourses: social interactions in academic writing.* Harlow: Longman.

Hyland, K. (2002) Authority and invisibility: authorial identity in academic writing. *Journal of Pragmatics* 34: 1091–112.

Johns, A. M. (1997) *Text, Role, and Context: developing academic literacies.* Cambridge: Cambridge University Press.

Jordan, R. R. (1990) *Academic Writing Course.* Harlow: Longman.

Kaplan, N. (1965) The norms of citation behaviour: prolegomena to the footnote. *American Documentation* 16: 181.

Latour, B. (1987) *Science in Action: how to follow scientists and engineers through society.* Milton Keynes: Open University Press.

Latour, B. and Woolgar, S. (1979) *Laboratory Life: the social construction of scientific facts.* Beverly Hills: Sage Publications.

Lea, M. R. and Stierer, B. (2000) Introduction to M. R. Lea and B. Stierer (eds) *Student Writing in Higher Education: new contexts*. 1–13. Buckingham: The Society for Research into Higher Education and Open University Press.

Lea, M. R. and Street, B. V. (2000) Student writing and staff feedback in higher education: an academic literacies approach. In M. R. Lea and B. Stierer (eds) *Student Writing in Higher Education: new contexts*. 32–46. Buckingham: The Society for Research into Higher Education and Open University Press.

Lillis, T. (1999) Whose 'common sense'? Essayist literacy and the institutional practice of mystery. In C. Jones et al. (eds) *Students Writing in the University*. 127–47. Amsterdam: John Benjamins.

MacRoberts, M. H. and MacRoberts, B. R. (1986) Quantitative measures of communication in science: a study of the formal level. *Social Studies of Science* 16: 151–72.

MacRoberts, M. H. and MacRoberts, B. R. (1996) Problems of citation analysis. *Scientometrics* 3(3): 435–44.

Matthews, J. R. et al (2000) *Successful Scientific Writing: a step-by-step guide for the biological and medical sciences* (second edition). Cambridge: Cambridge University Press.

Merton, R. K. (1968) The Matthew effect in science. *Science* 159, 5/1/1968: 56–63.

Moravcsik, M. J. and Murugesan, P. (1975) Some results on the function and quality of citations. *Social Studies of Science* 5: 86–92.

Newman, M. (2001) The academic achievement game: designs of undergraduates' efforts to get grades. *Written Communication* 18(4): 470–505.

Prior, P. A. (1998) *Writing/Disciplinarity: a sociohistoric account of literate activity in the academy*. Mahwah, NJ: Lawrence Erlbaum Associates.

Small, H. G. (1998) Citations and consillience in science. *Scientometrics* 43(1): 143–8.

Swales, J. M. and Feak, C. B. (1994) *Academic Writing for Graduate Students*. Ann Arbor: The University of Michigan Press.

Swales, J. M. and Feak, C. B. (2000) *English in Today's Research World: a writing guide*. Ann Arbor: The University of Michigan Press.

Thompson, G. and Hunston, S. (2000) Evaluation: an introduction. In S. Hunston and G. Thompson (eds) *Evaluation in Text: authorial stance and the construction of discourse*. 1–27. Oxford: Oxford University Press.

Thompson, P. (2001) A pedagogically-motivated corpus-based examination of PhD theses: macrostructure, citation practices and uses of modal verbs. Unpublished PhD thesis, University of Reading.

Thompson, P. and Tribble, C. (2001) Looking at citations: using corpora in English for academic purposes. *Language Learning and Technology* 5(3): 91–105.

Trzeciak, J. and MacKay, S. E. (1994) *Study Skills for Academic Writing.* New York: Prentice Hall.

Vinkler, P. (1987) A quasi-quantitative citation model. *Scientometrics* 12(1–2): 47–72.

Weissberg, R. and Buker, S. (1990) *Writing Up Research: experimental research report writing for students of English.* Englewood Cliffs: Prentice Hall Regents.

White, H. D. (2001) Authors as citers over time. *Journal of the American Society for Information Science and Technology* 52(2): 87–108.

Whitley, R. (2000) *The Intellectual and Social Organization of the Sciences* (second edition). Oxford: Oxford University Press.

7 The L2 learner corpus: reviewing its potential for the early stages of learning

Anne Ife

Anglia Polytechnic University

Abstract

The L2 learner corpus has been described as an idea 'whose hour has come'. On the other hand, its use has been confined largely to studies of advanced learners, usually learners of English, and to situations where an equivalent native-speaker corpus allows observation of degrees of 'non-nativeness'. The use of corpora with early learners has tended to be dismissed for a variety of reasons, including the variability of early production, the difficulties of tagging erroneous data, and the absence of suitable native-speaker corpora for comparison. This paper examines what use might realistically be made of a learner corpus in early L2 learning. It reports initial work with a corpus produced by multinational learners of Spanish as L2, taught in the same environment by the same teaching team. It examines the early acquisition of some core lexical items and provides indications from the corpus for the impact on acquisition of variables such as course materials and L1. We argue that, with available software, L2 corpora have a role to play in the early learning context, providing a useful research resource at the interface between research and teaching, especially in the area of vocabulary acquisition.

Introduction

In the world of corpus linguistics, the L2 learner corpus still feels like a relative newcomer. Described by Leech as an idea 'whose hour has come' (preface to Granger, 1998: xvi) it is nonetheless an idea that has been growing for a decade or more now and it is over 10 years since the start of the International Corpus of Learner English (ICLE, see Granger, 1994), one of the pioneers in the field. Among the growing body of learner corpora, English is well served (Granger, 1998; Milton & Chowdury, 1994; Liu & Shaw, 2001). However, there are now welcome signs of corpus projects focusing on other languages too (see Marsden et al., 2003; Cestero et al., 2002).

The present paper focuses on L2 Spanish learners and reports a corpus project designed to explore vocabulary development among adult learners of Spanish in the UK. It contextualises this work, prior to giving details of the corpus, and then illustrates, through a pilot study, the use that can be made of such a corpus. Finally it evaluates the corpus methodology used.

Background

This research has been stimulated by a number of factors linked with the increasing internationalisation of British higher education. Based in an international city (Cambridge) we found ourselves with nationally and linguistically varied groups of learners learning Spanish in the same classes, some progressing from ab initio level through to degree level four years later. This offered an unusual opportunity to observe the comparative progress of learners of different L1s in the early acquisition of Spanish.

Our specific interest is in lexical development and, referring to vocabulary acquisition, Meara (1996: 37) noted that there were 'in fact, very few studies which make comparisons between learners from different backgrounds acquiring the same L2'. A corpus methodology seemed to offer a potentially useful approach to studying the development of our learners. Although in sampling terms classes in any one year are relatively small (16–20), over several years we could have sizeable corpus to observe. What was needed was a way of making this a useful research tool – both for ourselves and for our postgraduate students.

Reference to other L2 corpus studies was rather discouraging. Firstly, a feature shared by many of the English projects is a focus on advanced learners. The ICLE corpus, for instance, consists of written texts gathered from advanced learners of English from countries across Europe: all were university students able to write substantial discursive texts in their L2. A major Hong Kong corpus (Milton & Chowdury, 1994) also uses data from learners whose English is adequate to enable them to begin university study in English.

A second common feature of studies based on these corpora is that they make use of parallel native-speaker corpora in order to assess the degree of nativeness or non-nativeness of the learners' interlanguage (see the collected papers in Granger, 1998; Liu & Shaw, 2001; Milton & Tsang, 1993). Learners' production can then be analysed to see how far it coincides with that produced by the similar group of native speakers.

The circumstances of our learners were very different since many were beginners or at most elementary learners. Clearly comparative studies can only be undertaken if a suitable corpus exists. With elementary levels of language development this is problematical since L1 users of the target language at similar stages of development are unlikely to form a comparable group with learners. They will be children, as yet cognitively undeveloped, and certainly not literate in writing skills. Even with a spoken language corpus, learners will mostly be older and inevitably more cognitively developed than children at equivalent stages of L1 development.

A third feature shared by the English studies is that they are frequently major projects, requiring a large investment of time, energy and resources for data collection, transcription and tagging. The literature also places heavy emphasis on the intricacies and laboriousness of internal tagging of texts and on the near absence of any such system for very erratic data. Meunier (1998: 21), citing Pieneman (1992) and Jagtman (1994), suggests that grammatical mark-up language for learner data may even need to be devised from scratch. Marsden et al. (2003) were able to use the CHILDES tools but at the same time stress the major investment of time required (2003: 109). Clearly for many individual researchers this is a major deterrent from undertaking corpus-based research at this level.

Amidst the deterrent comments in the literature, Granger (1998) does make more encouraging noises, stressing the value of teachers analysing learners' output with the help of computer techniques. Such an approach she says 'may well come up with highly interesting new insights based on quantitative information which may in itself not be statistically significant but which nevertheless has value within a pedagogical framework' (1998: 16). She also stresses that a computerised approach, although it has limitations, is ideally suited to the study of lexis, although she points out the need for computerised methods and manual methods to go hand in hand. She notes that learner corpora may be particularly valuable in the as yet unresolved question of the exact role of transfer.

Alongside this more encouraging perspective, the WordSmith Tools software was also now available. With its focus on the exploration of lexis, it was reasonably user-friendly and offered scope for the kind of investigation we wanted to do. We thus committed ourselves to the (still considerable) task of creating an electronically explorable learner corpus.

McNeill (1994) is sceptical of the potential value of corpora that are simply raw banks of data. Instead he advocates creating a corpus only of errors, since the large data-bank approach runs the risk of being data driven rather than research driven. However, we reject McNeill's advocacy of the error-only approach because it involves pre-judging the very issues we wished to observe. What we are interested in is how learners are building their early lexicons relative to each other, and what evidence there is of L1 transfer or of the impact of input. We are also concerned not so much with errors of form but with how learners **use** the words they acquire, the selections they make, the meanings they attach to them and how their lexicons are developing. Nonetheless, McNeill's point about data-driven rather than research-driven research is important. We accept that a corpus of L2 learner language will not in itself allow immediate breakthroughs in language acquisition research, but it may offer important potential for 'test-bed' research, a place where hunches can be explored and initial evidence sought that can then be pursued in more tailored research designs. We anticipate the need always for subsequent, research-driven designs.

To summarise our general research questions, what we were most interested to explore was:

- whether an L2 learner corpus is useful on a relatively small scale;
- whether it will provide useful information on low-proficiency learners with no suitable L1 groups for comparison;
- whether there is scope for working with an untagged corpus;
- what might be the advantages and limitations of corpus methodology.

In short, is this a methodology that can be used by small-scale researchers or classroom practitioners who may have their own research questions 'at the interface' between teaching and research?

The APU learner Spanish corpus

The texts

The corpus currently consists of written texts produced by our learners of Spanish over a period of about four years, some tracked from beginner to final year degree level. Beginners' texts are usually short (150–200 words long) and are mostly *descriptive* or *narrative* text types. More advanced outputs are usually around 500 words long. There is inevitably increased sophistication of text types as students' proficiency grows and advanced texts include more *argumentation, exposition, opinion, reporting* and less narrative and description. The corpus currently contains about 120,000 words, distributed as in Table 1.

Proficiency level	Number of texts
Beginners	190
Intermediate	35
Advanced 1/2	118
Advanced 3/4	17
Advanced 5/6	99

(Proficiency levels equate to hours of study and to descriptors used in teaching)

Table 1 Corpus contents (120,000 words approx)

Texts were produced either as coursework or as exam work. This distinction, plus text type and task-type are indicated in a text header. Precise details of the task are also given and can easily be accessed when searching the data. Since tasks are similar from year to year we have similar data from a good number of students.

The learners

So far 207 students are represented in the corpus. All are mainstream languages undergraduates. Also included are some ERASMUS students from France/Germany/Italy who continue study of Spanish while in England. Most of these students fall into the 'advanced' category.

In recent years at least 50 per cent of our languages students have been non-native speakers of English and this is reflected in the corpus. Half the students have English as L1, otherwise a number of nationalities and L1s are represented, mostly from Europe, but also including China and Japan. In all, 18 different L1s are represented, although several of these are isolated cases (Table 2). After English, French is the most common L1, most French students being ERASMUS students at the advanced stage. Italian is the next most common L1 and most of these are standard degree students who come as beginners in Spanish, as do the Greek, Finnish, Swedish, Russian, Chinese and Japanese speakers. The German speakers fall into both categories, the advanced usually being ERASMUS students, the beginners standard 'home' degree students. Details of L1 are included in the text header as is the sex of the learner and the student's unique ID number.

L1	Number of Ss
English	102
French	30
Italian	22
German	10
Greek	10
Japanese	6
Chinese	4
Finnish	4
Russian	4
Swedish	3
Other: one each of Portuguese, Czech, Turkish, Dutch, Danish, Luxemburgisch, Slavic, Ethiopian	8
Not known	4
Total	207

Table 2 L1s represented in the corpus

Searching via the text header

To summarise the data logged in the text header, this includes:

- task conditions (exam vs. coursework)
- specific task set
- text-type (description, narrative, argumentation, exposition, reporting, opinion)
- proficiency level (beginners, intermediate, advanced)
- L1
- sex of student
- coursebook
- ID number

Thus all texts, or subsets, can be searched according to any of the elements above, or according to combinations of them.

The software tools

The WordSmith Tools software (Scott, 1997) offers two potentially useful facilities for exploring vocabulary use in texts. Space precludes a detailed analysis here, but in brief the *Wordlist* facility gives considerable scope for examining learners' progress in terms of words actively used, for differentiating between learners in the use of the same vocabulary, and for assessing the success of tasks set in eliciting supposedly learned vocabulary. It also allows the observation of lexical variety and the lexical richness of learners' texts through type-token ratios and through increasing word and sentence length.

The *Concordancer* on the other hand allows examination of the use of individual words in context, making it feasible to see how learners are using words in context, what word-selection choices they are making and (with higher proficiency) to observe their collocational knowledge. There is scope for monitoring lexical development either in individuals or in subgroups of learners and even in relation to lexicogrammatical systems such as wh- words, prepositions, and articles.

The pilot study

Our pilot study has examined the acquisition of some core lexical items in early Spanish production. The words under focus were verbs that represent a three-way lexical split for English speakers and are a known cause of difficulty affecting primarily in word selection. This difficulty persists often into advanced stages of learning. Of interest to us was how these words are acquired by learners of a range of L1s in the early stages of development and we were interested to see whether learners of different mother tongues, given the same input, experience the same difficulties and go through similar learning processes. This will be reported in greater detail elsewhere. This paper will concentrate on one aspect of the study to show how the corpus has provided early insights into the teaching/learning process.

Broadly, the Spanish verbs in question equate to different aspects of the semantic spectrum covered by the verb 'to be' in English. Table 3 shows the form in which the verbs are encountered initially, together with their infinitival form and the key aspect of meaning encountered in the early L2 learning context.

Our focus was on primarily on word selection – not accuracy of form. The WordSmith concordancer revealed easily the context in which the learners used these words, providing quick reference back to the original text when necessary. Reassuringly, 70 per cent of selections were correct at the beginner stage under written assessment conditions but we were curious to know what happened in the other 30 per cent of cases.

Spanish example with English equivalent	Infinitival form of verb	Key semantic meaning in context learnt
Mi padre es taxista My father IS a taxi driver	*ser*	Identification
Madrid está en España Madrid IS in Spain	*estar*	Location
En mi ciudad hay una catedral In my town there IS a cathedral	*haber*	Existence/ Location

Table 3 Spanish verbs under observation

We shall here focus only on two of the verbs: *estar* and *haber* (most frequently encountered as *hay*). Table 3 shows that there is semantic overlap between these verbs. *Estar* is always assumed to be a potential cause of difficulty for learners whose mother tongue does not also require a special verb to indicate location, separate from the normal verb meaning 'to be'. On the other hand it is a word that is inevitably encountered early in the learning process. *Hay* is not often linked with it, although it too equates to English 'is' in the locational context as shown in the example. *Hay* is always used frequently in early classroom input and seems an intuitively simple word, with no major problems in its use, especially since it is invariable in the present tense, while *estar* has the usual Spanish verb morphology, varying according to person and number.

However, a major distinction between the two verbs is that *estar* is used when the referent is known, thus requiring a definite article, as in example (a) below, while *(haber) hay* is used when the existence of the referent is still being established. Thus it is used with the indefinite article, with numbers, or qualifiers like 'many', as in examples (b), (c) and (d) respectively.

a) *La catedral está en el centro* (THE cathedral is in the centre)

b) *En mi ciudad hay UNA catedral* (In my town there is A cathedral)

c) *En mi ciudad hay MUCHOS bancos* (In my town there are MANY banks)

d) *En esta calle hay TRES cines* (In this street there are THREE cinemas)

One course book we have used (Cerrolaza et al., 1998) is conscious of this distinction and presents the words together in the relevant contexts, contrasting them and emphasizing the definiteness / indefiniteness aspect. One of the others we have used (Universdad de Salamanca / Radiotelevisión española, 1991) maintains a distinction between the two and does not present them together at all.

In our corpus data, we found some clear evidence of students selecting *está* in contexts that required *hay*: in beginner texts there were 36 cases of this. But we found almost no cases the other way round (*hay* for *está*): only three out of 282 uses were erroneous choices of this sort. This was rather surprising because, as well as representing a meaning distinction that is usually new to speakers of other languages, *estar* is morphologically variable, like all Spanish verbs, and needs thought about its precise form.

Analysis of the students making this misselection revealed that 11 students (of 110) produced all the cases. Both English natives and speakers of other languages were involved (Table 4).

Student	Mother tongue	No of texts	Cases
A	Chinese	1	1
B	English	5	8
C	English	3	7
D	English	2	7
E	English	4	4
F	German	1	1
G	German	1	1
H	German	1	1
I	Greek	1	4
J	Italian	1	1
K	Japanese	1	1

Table 4 Misselection of *estar* for *haber* (*hay*)

Notable is the fact that four English speakers (students B, C, D, E) account for the majority (72 per cent) of occurrences. Indeed, they are 'repeat offenders' over several texts and two continue into the second semester. Other students produce mostly one case, except for a Greek student (I) who produces four in one text. This might suggest that L1 transfer plays a role here but in fact plenty of English L1 speakers among the learners do not make this misselection, so the question arises of what causes the confusion in the lexicons of these learners?

To begin with, the texts of these students showed them to be generally weak students overall. The student codes also reveal that the majority of the students who make this misselection (and all the English speakers) are from three intakes (1999–2001), which used the very course book that stresses the definiteness

/ indefiniteness distinction. Clearly not all the students in those intakes are affected – English L1 or otherwise – but something causes these particular students to overgeneralise *estar.*

This led us to look more closely at this course book and to consider again the overlap between *estar* and *haber* (*hay*). Closer comparison suggests more complexity in their relationship than we had hitherto supposed and it may begin to explain the direction of the over-generalisation (*está* for *hay* but not vice versa). This complexity can be summarised as follows:

- although morphologically variable, *estar* looks like a typical Spanish verb – whereas *hay* does not: it is morphologically unusual;
- *hay* lacks a plural form but the intended meaning may well involve plurality ('there are' as well as 'there is');
- *hay* is used only in third person while *estar* is used normally with all persons;
- the subject NP always follows *hay*; the subject NP <u>may</u> follow *estar*;
- *hay* needs no pro-form like the English 'there'.

Detailed inspection of the course book found that, although the distinction between *hay* and *estar* was presented clearly initially, there was then little reinforcement or recycling of *hay* with the indefinite article and, in fact, relatively little use of *hay* overall (62 cases).

More significantly perhaps, the contexts in which *estar* occurred (50) mirrored the structure of *hay*, with a following subject NP (V + subject NP) which is actually the marked form for *estar*. At the same time there were few uses of the more normal unmarked structure with a preceding subject NP: NP V (Adv) : *el/la X está...* (= *the X is...*).

Examples of *está* usually occurred in questions = Q + V + NP:

¿Dónde está el Palacio Real? Where is the Royal Palace?

¿Dónde está la calle Atocha? Where is Atocha [Street]?

or in sentences with adverbial preceding V and NP following: Adv + V + NP:

Muy cerca está el Museo del Prado

Very close is the Prado (= The Prado is very close)

Allí está el puente

There is the bridge (= The bridge is there)

Al lado del 'super' está la farmacia, ¿no?

Beside the supermarket is the chemist's, right?

Inversion of verb and subject might not be surprising in questions, but this second set represent a much more marked structure.

Furthermore, when NP precedes *estar* in the course book, the definite article (the distinguishing feature for *estar* compared with *hay*) is often distanced from *estar* by intervening adjectival or prepositional phrases:

A escuela más cercana está...

The school most near is (the nearest school is...)

La mayoría de los cines están en el centro

The majority of the cinemas are in the centre

All these factors mean that learners see *estar* and *hay* in the same structural / meaning frame (with a following NP) before they have got used to the definiteness / indefiniteness association of each in distinct contexts and frames: thus the potential help of a distinct structural frame is denied to them. In this context it may be less surprising that they choose the word that seems more typical of Spanish verbs (*estar*) over the apparently simple *hay*.

The corpus data showed that learners taught with the other course book, which maintains a clear separation of the two, and presents more unmarked examples of *estar*, did not seem to show this confusion. While the course book does not represent the only input it is the most permanent source available to learners.

Our findings on the basis of this study cannot of course be conclusive. However, they suggest a need to treat the early learning of these two words with some caution. In the way that it is not advisable to teach synonyms on the same occasion, verbs like these that share semantic features but show distinct syntactic features may need consolidating separately, especially for weaker learners.

Conclusions

We have tried to illustrate here how our corpus has given us a retrospective overview of one aspect of our students' learning. It would be untrue to suggest that creating the corpus did not require a considerable commitment of time and energy, including the time to learn the software. We regard this, however, as time well spent and the task of updating the corpus should be relatively easy, especially since there are ways of collecting learner outputs electronically and retaining the original format of their writing, even when these are also corrected electronically. The fact that learners may use spell checks on their work, or even grammar checks, will not invalidate the type of approach we are taking, which involves students' lexical choices rather than errors of form or syntax.

We do not make over-large claims for the corpus and have already stated that findings, to be more conclusive, need to be followed up by focused research designs. However, we do see it as a valuable resource in the generation of research topics and as an aid in speeding up some of the early stages of research project design. It can also help in contexts where learners of the target language are not numerous, which is one disadvantage researchers in this county have when working on languages other than English.

The corpus is also useful, as we said before, 'at the interface' between research and teaching. As teachers we have found insights into our learners' early development. As materials writers we can also benefit from these insights, not only in understanding better how to present new items but also in observing how learners are trying to express themselves. We can respond to this by devising better tasks to assist them in reaching their goals.

In short, we feel that the L2 learner corpus is worthwhile, even at the early stages of learning, as long as it is viewed realistically and not expected to provide all the answers either to researchers or teachers; rather it can act as a useful adjunct as a ready source of real data produced by real learners, which can be very difficult to come by in the normal teaching / research context.

References

Cerrolaza, M., Cerrolaza, O. and Llovet, B. (1998) *Planet@E.L.E.*, Madrid: Edelsa.

Cestero Mancera, A. M., Penadés Martínez, I., Blanco Canales, A., Camargo Fernández, L. and Simón Granda, J. (2002) Corpus para el análisis de errores de aprendices de ELE (CORANE). A. M. Gimeno Sanz (ed.) *Tecnologías de la información y de las comunicaciones en la enseñanza de ELE*. 527–34. Universidad Politécnica de Valencia.

Granger, S. (1994) The learner corpus: a revolution in applied linguistics. *English Today* 39: 25–9.

Granger, S. (1998) (ed.) *Learner English on Computer*. London & New York: Addison Wesley Longman.

Jagtman, M. (1994) COMOLA – a computer system for the analysis of interlanguage data. *Second Language Research* 10(1): 49–83.

Liu, E.T.K. and Shaw, P. M. (2001) Investigating learners' vocabulary. *International Review of Applied Linguistics in Language Teaching* 39(3): 171–94.

McNeill, A. (1994) A corpus of learner errors: making the most of a database. In L. Flowerdew and K. K. Tong (eds) *Entering Text*. 114–125. The Hong Kong University of Science and Technology: Hong Kong.

Marsden, E., Myles, F., Rule, S. and Mitchell, R. (2003) Using CHILDES tools for researching second language acquisition. In S. Sarangi and T. van Leeuwen *Applied Linguistics and Communities of Practice*. 98–113. London & New York: BAAL/Continuum.

Meara, P. (1996) The classical research in L2 vocabulary acquisition. In G. Anderman and M. Rodgers *Words, Words, Words*. 27–40. Multilingual Matters: Clevedon.

Meunier, F. (1998) Computer tools for the analysis of learner corpora. In Granger (1998). 19–37.

Milton, J. and Chowdury, N. (1994) Tagging the interlanguage of Chinese learners of English. In L. Flowerdew and K. K. Tong (eds) *Entering Text*. 127–43. The Hong Kong University of Science and Technology: Hong Kong.

Milton, J. and Tsang, E. (1993) A corpus-based study of logical connectors in EFL students' writing. In R. Pemberton and E. Tsang (eds) *Studies in Lexis*. 215–26. The Hong Kong University of Science and Technology: Hong Kong.

Pieneman, M. (1992) COALA – a computational system for interlanguage analysis. *Second Language Research* 8(1): 59–92.

Scott, M. and Oxford University Press (1997) *WordSmith Tools*, Oxford University Press.

Universidad de Salamanca and Radiotelevisión Española (1991) *Viaje al español*. Madrid: Santillana.

8 Composing competence: How L1 and L2 writing experience interact

Hiroe Kobayashi and Carol Rinnert

Hiroshima University and Hiroshima City University

Abstract

Previous studies of expert vs. novice L2 writers have investigated the influence of L1 or L2 experience, but not of their combined effects on the writing of novice writers. This study examines possible interaction between L1 (Japanese) and L2 (English) writing experience, particularly special preparatory high school training in writing short essays for university entrance exams. First-year Japanese university students, all with intermediate level EFL proficiency and having no university-level L2 writing instruction, formed four groups with: (1) intensive experience writing essays in both L1 and L2, (2) only L1 experience, (3) only L2 experience, and (4) no such experience. Students with only L1 experience wrote well-organized, coherent essays, but included little support or elaboration; those with only L2 training included relatively elaborated support for their points, but showed little sense of overall essay structure; and students with no training tended to use the kind of self-reflective writing they learned as children. In contrast, students with both L1 and L2 experience wrote significantly longer essays that were more coherently structured and developed with richly elaborated support, suggesting that acquisition of composing competence may be facilitated by the combination of L1 and L2 writing experience.

Introduction

To help inexperienced student writers become more like 'experts', numerous studies have sought to identify strategies the experts use in their composing process (Hayes, Flower, Schriver, Stratman & Carey, 1987; Cumming, 1989; Sasaki, 2000, 2002). These studies found that expert writers, either in a first (L1) or a second language (L2), employ more effective planning and revising strategies than novices. The assumption underlying these studies is that expert and novice writers exist on a single continuum (Carter, 1990; Grabe & Kaplan, 1996), and that novice writers can approximate the performance of experts by learning the strategies of those skilled writers and applying them to their own writing.

From a cognitive perspective, an expert can be considered to be a writer having 'the ability to employ certain universal, context-independent revision and editing practices to guide writing' (Hyland, 2002: 59). Attaining such ability appears to involve a number of variables, including text knowledge, in relation to which writing experience appears to play a major role. In fact, in writing research (Cumming, 1989; Hayes et al., 1987; Sasaki, 2002), expert writers are often referred to as 'professionally experienced writers,' while novice writers are defined as writers who have little or no writing training or experience.

In discussing 'writing experience' in relation to the concept of an expert/novice writer, second language writing research entails at least two issues. One is concerned with the amount of experience student writers have writing in either L1 or L2 or both, and the other is related to levels of second language proficiency. First, the effect of L1 writing experience on L2 writing appears to be positive (Bosher, 1998; Cohen & Brooks-Carson, 2001; Cumming, 1989; Raimes, 1987; Uzawa, 1996). Cumming (1989), for example, found that French-speaking university students with extensive professional L1 writing experience produced L2 (English) essays with effective content and discourse organization, while attending to complex aspects of writing and employing problem-solving strategies. In his study, Cumming did not find any obvious effect of second language proficiency on such writing processes. Similarly, Raimes (1987) found that there was little correlation between language proficiency and composing strategies of L2 students; however, those with confidence in their L1 writing ability revised and edited most frequently. The findings of these studies suggest that writing ability and language proficiency are independent from each other, and at the same time that L1 writing ability, which is presumably at least partially constituted of L1 writing experience, is transferable to L2 writing.

Amount and kinds of L2 writing experience have also been found to affect the quality of writing and composing strategies. For example, L2 students with paragraph writing experience in high school were found to be better writers than those without such experience (Sasaki & Hirose, 1996). Likewise, L2 students with more experience of writing short and longer texts were better able than less experienced students to detect and correct problems at three discourse levels: intersentential, paragraph and essay (Kobayashi & Rinnert, 2001). In terms of composing strategies, Sasaki (2000; 2002) found that L2 expert writers made more detailed overall plans for organization and refined their texts more frequently than the novices, who tended to make less detailed plans and make corrections and translations at a local level. Although these findings suggest a positive correlation between L2 writing experience and L2 writing performance, caution should be urged because writing experience and language proficiency are often inseparable due to a high degree of overlap between the two factors (Kobayashi & Rinnert, 2001).

The study

Previous studies have investigated the effect of either L1 or L2 writing experience on second language writing. However, hardly any studies have attempted to examine the direct effects of both L1 and L2 writing experience or possible interaction between the two. Furthermore, previous studies have tended not to pay sufficient attention to social contexts (Roca De Larios, Murphy & Martin, 2002). Since writing takes place in a situated context, the writing practice writers receive in their L1 literacy setting is likely to affect their writing behaviors.

The goal of this study is to explore possible interaction between L1 (Japanese) and L2 (English) writing experience. In particular, we focus on the effects of special preparatory high school level training in writing short essays in both languages for university entrance examinations. A previous study (Kobayashi & Rinnert, 2002) identified such training as a potentially influential factor affecting the quality of Japanese students' English writing after entering university. Although the overall current study aims to examine effects on both L1 and L2 writing, this paper presents only those results relating to L2 English writing.

The special preparatory training, which students experienced during their last year of high school, consisted of one to three months of intensive, individualized instruction (e.g., one-to-one between teacher and student after regular school hours). For both L1 and L2, the students who received such intensive training wrote 10 to 12 essays, received feedback on them from their teachers and then revised them on the basis of the feedback. For both languages, unlike the traditional L1 composition training which focuses on the expression of personal thoughts and feelings (Watanabe, 2001)[1], the special training geared for university entrance essay exams tended to emphasize the importance of stating a position (usually at the beginning) and supporting the position with specific evidence. The main differences in the preparation in the two languages related to the length of the writing, which reflected the entrance examination specifications at universities that required essay writing. For the L1 training, students were instructed to write multi-paragraph Japanese essays that included an introduction, body and conclusion. For the L2 training, they were required to write only single 80 to 100-word paragraphs.

The specific research questions addressed in this paper are the following:

1. Does writing fluency differ among writers in the four groups (those with preparatory training in both L1 and L2 writing, those with training in only L1, those with training in only L2, and those with no training)?

2. How do text features (overall structure, development of content) vary among writers in the four groups?

Method

The participants were all Japanese first-year university EFL students (N=19). Because none of them had received any university-level L2 writing instruction, they could be considered novice EFL writers. Their English proficiency was held constant at an intermediate level, as shown in Table 1. The participants were selected to form four groups:

1. Group 1, those with intensive experience writing essays in both L1 and L2 (N = 8);

2. Group 2, those with experience writing in only L1 (N = 4);

3. Group 3, those with experience in only L2 (N = 4);

4. Group 4, those with no experience in either language (N = 3).[2]

	Number	Preparatory training	English mean score* (SD)	
Group 1	8	L1 & L2	468.13	(18.60)
Group 2	4	L1 only	462.75	(45.54)
Group 3	4	L2 only	452.50	(20.08)
Group 4	3	Little or none	459.67	(5.13)

* TOEFL equivalent; no significant difference among groups

Table 1 Characteristics of participant groups

Each student wrote one Japanese and one English essay. The two open-ended opinion eliciting prompts were formulated as follows:

Topic 1: Place to live

Students at universities often have a chance to choose where to live. They may choose to live in an apartment alone near their school, or they may choose to live with their family and commute to their university. What do you think of this topic? Write an essay in English, explaining your opinion about it. Your written essay will be included in a compilation of class essays and your classmates will read it.

Topic 2: Travel

Many university students love to travel. They may choose to travel alone, or they may choose to travel in a group. What do you think of this topic? Write an essay in English, explaining your opinion about it. Your written essay will be included in a compilation of class essays and your classmates will read it.

All participants composed essays and engaged in individual in-depth interviews in two separate sessions, writing in Japanese during their first session and in English during their second one. The topics were alternated, with half of the students in each group writing on Topic 1 in Japanese and on Topic 2 in English, and the other half doing the opposite. No time limit was given, but most participants took about 35 minutes to write each essay in either L1 or L2. They were allowed to use electronic dictionaries for their L2 writing.

After each essay was completed, students answered in-depth questions about their composing processes (for example, how much they had planned before actually writing) and about their L1 and L2 writing background. Each interview session lasted between 90 and 120 minutes.

The data were analyzed in terms of both writing process and writing product. Here we report on the findings regarding writing fluency and text analysis. The composing behavior of the participants was analyzed in an attempt to measure their writing fluency based on a count of the number of words produced, measurement of the time taken to write, and calculation of the number of words/minute. The textual analysis included relatively well-established analyses of text structure, organization and coherence (e.g., Hirose, 2003; Kubota, 1998; Sasaki, 2000), as explained under Results, below. In addition, special attention was paid to the development and elaboration of the content in the written texts. Based on modified versions of PISA, Procedure for Incremental Structure Analysis (Sanders & van Wijk, 1996), and TRACE, Text-based Reconstructions of Activities by the Conceptual Executive (van Wijk, 1999), the texts were segmented into basic meaning units and coded in terms of their contribution to the argument or exposition. According to their theory (van Wijk, 1999), the basic components of an argument essay can be represented as follows:

> Argument → *Claim* + (*Support*)
> *Support* → *Reason* + (*Elaboration*) [RECURSIVE]
> *Reason* → characteristic / motivation / cause / ...
> *Elaboration* –> *Context* / *Specification* / *Nuancing* / ...
> *Context* → background / condition / evidence / ...
> *Specification* → characteristic / consequence / example / ...
> *Nuancing* → alternative / concession / contrast / ...

(based on van Wijk, 1999: 48)

(See Sanders & van Wijk (1996) and van Wijk (1999) for detailed explanation and examples of their segmentation and categorization criteria.) We attempted to follow their basic approach, but we added several new categories, based on patterns that emerged from our own data. These included the category of *metadiscourse* to identify those segments that functioned to signal major structural components of the overall essay and the categories of *extended explanation* and *extended nuancing* to distinguish the deeper elaboration of a single, complex point from a listing of simple parallel points.

Appendix 1 shows the segmentation and categorization of a sample essay from Group 2. The segments are numbered (with syntactically subordinate segments indicated with the letter *a*), and the category codes are listed to the right of each segment. Two raters (the authors) separately coded four out of the 19 essays (20 per cent of the data) and achieved an acceptable agreement rate of 58 out of 64 segmentation decisions (90.6 per cent); the remaining essays were coded separately and any disagreements were resolved through discussion.

Results

The results of the fluency measures, shown in Table 2 indicate that Group 1 wrote more words, at a faster rate, than the other three groups. According to independent *t*-tests, Group 1 students, who had received intensive training in both L1 and L2 (N = 8), wrote significantly longer English essays ($t = 2.717$, *df* = 17, $p = .015$) at a significantly faster rate ($t = 1.780$, *df* = 17, $p = .093$)[3] than the students in the other three groups combined (N = 11), who had received training in only one language or no training in either language.

	Word count	Words/Minute
	Mean (SD)	Mean (SD)
Group 1	193.88** (48.47)	6.28* (2.28)
Group 2	127.25 (20.84)	4.74 (2.48)
Group 3	151.00 (37.14)	4.27 (1.70)
Group 4	157.67 (35.95)	4.88 (1.60)

$**p < .05, *p < .1$

Table 2 Fluency: word length and rate of writing

Table 3 summarizes the most salient features that were found to distinguish among the texts of the four groups, each of which is explained below.

	Rhetorical pattern	Overall essay structure and coherence markers	Development of ideas
Group 1 **(N = 8)**	Mostly argumentation	Use of both meta-discourse markers and inter-paragraph markers Wide variety of inter-sentential connectors	Many reasons with highly elaborated support More general than personal evidence
Group 2 **(N = 4)**	All argumentation	Use of both meta-discourse markers and inter-paragraph markers At least three paragraphs including introduction, body and conclusion	Well-developed introduction Underdeveloped body (listing reasons without much elaboration) Somewhat developed conclusion
Group 3 **(N = 4)**	Mostly argumentation	No use of meta-discourse makers Minimal use of inter-paragraph markers Variety of inter-sentential connectors	Relatively many reasons with elaborated support More personal than general evidence

Group 4 (N = 3)	Mostly self-reflection	No use of meta-discourse markers Minimal use of inter-paragraph markers	Few reasons with rich elaboration More personal than general evidence

Table 3 Salient characteristics of texts by group

(1) Organizational and rhetorical patterns

Three basic rhetorical patterns were identified in the essays: *argumentation* (taking one side and giving supporting reasons, with or without a counter-argument), *exposition* (analyzing the topic in terms of its components or factors) and *self-reflection* (thinking about the topic from a personal perspective). Argumentation was the most common pattern for Groups 1 and 3 (appearing in 87 per cent of Group 1 essays and 75 per cent of Group 3 essays) and the only pattern for Group 2 (100 per cent); exposition was found in only four essays (three in Group 1 and one in Group 3), and self-reflection appeared to be preferred by Group 4 (occurring in 66 per cent of their essays), whereas it appeared in only one other essay (by a member of Group 1).[4]

Regarding the overall structure, the Group 2 essays all contained clearly identifiable introduction, body and conclusion paragraphs, whereas the other groups produced more varied structures. For example, two of the four Group 3 essays, three of the eight Group 1 essays and one of three Group 4 essays contained no identifiable introductory paragraphs.

In terms of inductive vs. deductive development of ideas, a majority (12 of 19) of the essays were developed deductively, with the thesis statement coming at or near the beginning of the essay; four essays (three of them by members of Group 1) were developed inductively, with a thesis statement coming at the end; and two could be described as being developed 'quasi-inductively' (Hinds, 1990), with a delayed statement of purpose in the form of a thesis statement occurring in the middle of the essay.[5]

(2) Discourse and coherence markers

Striking inter-group differences were seen in the use of meta-discourse segments (explicit markers of overall essay structure), which appeared in 75 per cent of both Group 1 and Group 2 essays, but in none of the Group 3 or 4 essays. Similarly, inter-paragraph transition markers, such as *First, On the other hand*, and *Finally*, occurred in all of the essays by Group 1 and in 75 per cent of those by Group 2, but in only one of the essays by each of the other two groups.

Although inter-sentential connectors appeared in almost every essay, the quality and variety of connectors varied across the four groups. In the Group 4 essays, the only connectors used were *And, But* and *So*. Although these three also occurred frequently in essays by members of the other groups, a much richer variety appeared in Group 1, including *Above all, Besides, For example, In addition to that, In fact, In short,* and *However,* and to a lesser extent in Group 3, who used *Also, In fact, However,* and *Therefore,* and Group 2, who used *For example,* and *However.*

(3) Development of content

The development of ideas in the body of the essays was analyzed by identifying (1) the number of reasons given, and (2) to what extent the reasons were supported in the form of elaboration (based mainly on van Wijk, 1999, as explained under Method). Table 4 displays the means and standard deviations of the number of reasons per essay; the number of segments in each of four categories of elaboration that were identified: *context* (conditions, background), *specification* (examples, characteristics, consequences), *nuancing* (contrasts, concessions, alternatives), and *evaluation* (relative value in comparison with other reasons); the total number of segments devoted to elaboration; and the ratio of elaboration segments per reason for the essays in each group.

		Category of elaboration					
Group	Reasons	Context	Specification	Nuancing	Evaluation	Total elab. frequency	Elab. segments per reason
1 (N=8) 4.63 (2.07)	I:*	1.75 (1.49)	4.50 (2.08)	0.50 (0.76)	0.25 (0.46)	7.00 (2.62)	
	S:**	2.38 (2.39)	10.38 (5.48)	0.75 (1.04)	0.25 (0.46)	13.75 (6.88)	(3.87 (2.84)
2 (N=4) 2.25 (0.50)	I:	0.25 (0.50)	1.25 (1.26)	0.50 (0.58)	0.00 (0.00)	2.00 (1.16)	
	S:	0.25 (0.50)	2.75 (3.59)	0.50 (0.58)	0.00 (0.00)	3.50 (3.11)	1.63 (1.60)
3 (N=4) 3.50 (1.92)	I:	3.25 (1.89)	3.25 (2.36)	0.25 (0.50)	0.25 (0.50)	7.00 (1.41)	
	S:	3.25 (1.89)	4.50 (3.70)	0.25 (0.50)	0.25 (0.50)	8.25 (2.75)	2.92 (1.83)
4 (N=3) 1.50 (0.71)	I:	2.00 (1.41)	1.00 (0.00)	0.50 (0.71)	0.00 (0.00)	3.50 (2.12)	
	S:	3.50 (0.79)	1.00 (0.00)	1.00 (1.41)	0.00 (0.00)	5.50 (0.71)	4.00 (1.41)

Table 4 Numbers of supporting reasons and elaboration: means (SDs) by group

As shown in Table 4, on average, Groups 1 and 3 gave twice as many reasons as Groups 2 and 4. The most salient group differences in terms of categories of elaboration included the greater amount of *specification* by Group 1 (with means of 4.5 instances and 10.38 segments per essay) and to a lesser extent Group 3 (with 3.25 instances and 4.5 segments) as compared to the other two groups (who ranged from 1 to 1.25 instances and from 1 to 2.75 segments), and the relatively much less frequent use of *context* by Group 2 (0.25 as opposed to means of 1.75 to 3.50 for the other 3 groups).

Similar distinctions can be seen among the groups in terms of the amount of total elaboration. Groups 1 and 3 provided many more total instances of elaboration than Groups 2 and 4 (means of 7.00 for both of the former, and 2.00 and 3.50, respectively, for the latter), and Group 1 had a remarkably larger number of segments of elaboration (13.75) as compared to Groups 2, 3 and 4 (with 3.50, 8.25 and 5.50, respectively). Groups 1, 3 and 4 all out-scored Group 2 in terms of the mean number of elaboration segments per reason (a range of 2.92 to 4.00 vs. only 1.63 for Group 2). However, considering that Group 4 gave relatively few reasons (with a mean of only 1.5 per essay), as opposed to the other groups, this last apparent similarity has to be treated cautiously.

We also looked at the use of personal (as opposed to general) evidence to support the points in the essays. Whereas personal (self-centered) experience was included in 100 per cent of the essays by members of Group 3 and 4, it was used in 75 per cent of Group 2 and only 50 per cent of Group 1 essays.

Discussion and conclusions

Students with both L1 and L2 training (Group 1) were the most fluent writers. They also wrote the most well-developed and coherently structured essays, with a focus on the body, including elaboration to support their position, and a rich variety of coherence markers, including meta-discourse and inter-paragraph markers such as *First, In addition, However,* and *On the other hand* (see Appendix 2). In contrast, while the students with only L1 training (Group 2) also wrote relatively well-organized, coherent essays including an acknowledgement of the other side's argument, unlike Group 1, they tended to create proportionately overly elaborated introductions and to develop relatively little detail in the body of their essays. These students appeared to follow what they had learned in their L1 essay writing training, particularly regarding overall organization and inclusion of the other side's opinion, but they were not able to develop sufficient detail, probably due to their lack of L2 writing practice.

On the other hand, the students with only L2 training (Group 3) tended to include relatively elaborated support for their points, but unlike the first two groups, they showed little sense of overall essay or paragraph structure, displaying only minimal use of inter-paragraph markers and no meta-discourse markers. Although their focused paragraph-length L2 writing practice may have allowed them to develop the schema of points followed by explanation, this group of students appeared to lack meta-discourse knowledge, including awareness of overall essay structure and the need for discourse markers. Finally, those with no training often fell back on the kind of self-reflective writing they learned in elementary and junior high school, e.g., depending heavily on personal experience to convey their ideas.

These results clearly indicate that students with both L1 and L2 specialized writing training wrote L2 essays of better quality than those with only L1 or L2 or without training, which at the same time suggests that the interaction between L1 and L2 writing experience leads to qualitatively more beneficial effects than the sum of the separate effects of L1 and L2. There are several possible reasons to explain why such positive interaction tended to occur.

First, the increased amount of writing practice the students obtained from L1 and L2 could have helped to bridge the gap between 'declarative' and 'procedural' knowledge (Anderson, 1983), that is, to activate the linguistic and discourse knowledge they have acquired and apply it in their L2 writing. In the special preparatory training, which was usually individualized instruction, students often wrote an essay after reading a newspaper article and revised the essay based on feedback they received from their teacher (Kobayashi & Rinnert, 2002). Following this process, the students in the current study reported practising L1 and L2 writing at least ten times or more in each language. In this repeated performance, they not only gained knowledge about writing essays, but also practised how to apply it in actual writing.

Another reason may be that the relatively extensive experience of writing in both languages seems to encourage a strong sense of audience and the need to communicate with the reader convincingly. The kind of writing students practised for in the intensive training had a real audience, whom they had to convince in order to be accepted into the university they hoped to enter. Under such pressure, they were strongly motivated to write essays as clearly as possible for the reader. In the interviews, all Group 1 students reported having made such efforts, namely, by consciously using discourse markers for logical connections and also including examples and specific information for explanation.

Moreover, intensive experience in both languages appears to build the confidence to write longer, more detailed texts, and perhaps experiment with a variety of more complex arguments. Such experience evidently leads to an ability to attend both to the overall structure of the essay and to the development of ideas. It also appears to provide a sense of balance in terms of essay parts; that is, the introduction and conclusion tended to be shorter than the body, rather than either the introduction or conclusion dominating the essay in terms of length, as sometimes occurred in texts by those who had experienced only L1, L2 or no training.

Last, intensive experience in both languages may raise students' awareness of the differences in writing in L1 and L2, which could lead to the cultivation of a variety of strategies to cope with the difficulties of writing in L2. Such strategies reported by Group 1 students in the interviews included eliminating possible 'digressions' from the topic, writing directly in English, and converting ideas into simpler Japanese structures before translating them into English.

For all these reasons, the benefits the Group 1 students in this study received from their combined L1 and L2 writing experience apparently far exceeded those that the other two groups obtained from either L1 or L2 experience alone. It remains to be determined whether these findings from this small-scale exploratory study can be confirmed with a larger group of novice writers. If so, writing teachers may be encouraged to take advantage of the potential for transfer of writing ability across languages to help students develop their composing competence.

Acknowledgement

This study was supported by a research grant from the Japan Society for the Promotion of Science. We would like to express our gratitude to Michiko Kasuya and Junko Seto for their assistance in collecting the data and to Richard C. Parker for creating the tables.

Notes

1. In Japanese classes particularly in elementary school, students are encouraged to write their personal feelings and thoughts freely based on 'the shared experience of a teacher and fellow students' about school events such as a school trip or a sports meeting (Watanabe, 2001, p. 42). They are also often given an assignment to keep a diary and the teacher usually gives comments on its content. In junior and senior high school, however, the amount of writing students do tends to decrease and they do expressive writing less frequently (see Kobayashi & Rinnert, 2002).

2. Of the original four participants with no intensive writing training, one had to be dropped from the study because it was determined that she had

acquired English writing instruction after entering university and before writing the essays for this study.

3. Considering the very small number of participants, a significance level of $p < .1$ was considered acceptable.

4. It should be noted that four of the 19 essays were found to contain more than one pattern, three of them combining exposition with either argumentation or self-reflection (all in Group 1) and one combining argumentation with self-reflection (in Group 4).

5. The remaining essay, which was basically a narrative, was developed chronologically and could not be considered either deductive or inductive.

References

Anderson, J. R. (1983) *The Architecture of Cognition.* Cambridge, MA: Harvard University Press.

Bosher, S. (1998) The composing processes of three South East Asian writers at the post-secondary level: an explanatory study. *Journal of Second Language Writing* 7: 205–41.

Carter, M. (1990) The idea of expertise: an exploration of cognitive and social dimensions of writing. *College Composition and Communication* 41: 265–86.

Cohen, A. D. and Brooks-Carson, A. (2001) Research on direct vs. translated writing processes: implications for assessment. *Modern Language Journal* 85: 169–88.

Cumming, A. (1989) Writing expertise and second-language proficiency. *Language Learning* 39: 81–141.

Grabe, W. and Kaplan, R. (1996) *Theory and Practice of Writing.* New York: Longman.

Hayes, J. R., Flower, L., Shriver, K. A., Stratman, J. F. and Carey, L. (1987) Cognitive process in revision. In S. Rosenberg (ed.) *Advances in Applied Psycholinguistics.* Vol. 2. 176–240. New York: Cambridge University Press.

Hinds, J. (1990) Inductive, deductive, quasi-inductive: expository writing in Japanese, Korean, Chinese and Thai. In U. Connor and A. Jones (eds) *Coherence in Writing.* 81–109. Alexandria, VA: TESOL.

Hirose, K. (2003) Comparing L1 and L2 organizational patterns in the argumentative writing of Japanese EFL students. *Journal of Second Language Writing* 12(1): 181–209.

Hyland, K. (2002) *Teaching and Researching Writing.* New York: Pearson Education.

Kobayashi and Rinnert (2001) Factors relating to EFL writers' discourse level revision skills. *International Journal of English Studies* 1: 71–102.

Kobayashi, H. and Rinnert, C. (2002) High school student perceptions of first language literacy instruction: implications for second language writing. *Journal of Second Language Writing* 11(2): 91–116.

Kubota, R. (1998) An investigation of Japanese and English L1 essay organization: differences and similarities. *The Canadian Modern Language Review* 54: 475–507.

Raimes, A. (1987) Language proficiency, writing ability, and composing strategies: a study of ESL college students writers. *Language Learning* 37: 439–69.

Roca De Larios, J., Murphy, L. and Martin, J. (2002) A critical examination of L2 writing process research. In S. Ransdell and M. Barbier (eds) *New Directions for Research in L2 Writing*. 11–47. Boston: Kluwer Academic Publishers.

Sanders, T. and van Wijk, C. (1996) PISA – a procedure for analyzing the structure of explanatory texts. *Text* 16(1): 91–132.

Sasaki, M. (2000) Toward an empirical model of EFL writing processes: an exploratory study. *Journal of Second Language Writing* 9: 259–91.

Sasaki, M. (2002) Building an empirically-based model of EFL learners' writing processes. In S. Ransdell and M. Barbier (eds) *New Directions for Research in L2 Writing*. 49–80. Boston: Kluwer Academic Publishers.

Sasaki, M. and Hirose, K. (1996) Explanatory variables for EFL students' expository writing. *Language Learning* 46(1): 137–74.

Uzawa, K. (1996) Second language learners' processes of L1 writing, L2 writing, and translation from L1 into L2. *Journal of Second Language Writing* 5: 271–94.

van Wijk, C. (1999) Conceptual processes in argumentation: a developmental perspective. In M. Torrance and D. Galbraith (eds) *Knowing What to Write: conceptual processes in text production*. 31–50. Amsterdam: Amsterdam University Press.

Watanabe, M. (2001) *Sakubun shidou ni miru kosei to souzouryoku no paradokkusu: nichibei shotoukyoiku hikaku kara* [A paradox of individuality and creativity through composition lessons: a comparison of Japanese and American Elementary Schools]. *Journal of Educational Sociology* 69: 23–42.

9   Frame shifting and identity construction during whole class instruction: teachers as initiators and respondents in play frames

Vally Lytra

Dept. of Byzantine and Modern Greek Studies
King's College, London

Abstract

While 'sail[ing] with the framing winds' (Tannen, 1986: 92) appears to be the norm in Whole Class Instruction (henceforth WCI), in this paper, I explore frame shifts from instructional frames (e.g. lesson frames, class management frames) to play frames. The data consist of instructional interactions between a group of Greek-speaking monolingual and Greek-Turkish bilingual fourth graders and their teachers that took place in a mainstream primary school in Athens, Greece. Drawing on insights from interactional sociolinguistics and conversation analysis complemented by ethnographic data on classroom practices, I explore teacher-led shifts to play frames (e.g. teasing, joking) and the pupil uptakes they elicit as well as teacher responses to pupil-initiated play frames. This study illustrates that teachers afford a limited role to play frames during WCI and that they exploit them as a resource, mainly on specific occasions (i.e. in assessments and sequences of reproach). Moreover, the investigation of frame shifts to play and their subsequent uptakes can provide insights into how teachers and pupils vie to control locally the discursive interaction and how they engage in 'identity work' in the classroom.

Introduction

More recent approaches to classroom talk have probed into the heterogeneity of classroom discourses and have explored the social practices within which their production, dissemination and consumption are situated (e.g. Candela, 1999; Gutiérrez et al., 1999; Haworth, 1999; Maybin, 1994; 2003; Kambarelis, 2001). These studies have looked at how teachers and pupils exploit different genres, styles, registers (and, as I will argue in this paper, frames) across various settings (e.g. WCI, small group instruction, informal pupil-pupil talk) to generate heterogeneous and dynamic interactions and construct various social identities, roles and types of knowledge in the classroom.[1] In this context, studies of humour and the burlesque (including mimicry and parody of teachers' voices) in the classroom have looked into the role of humour and the burlesque as an interpersonal resource used by both teachers and pupils to negotiate multiple and potentially conflicting identities during instruction (Baynham, 1996; Hirst, 2003).

Taking this line of research as a point of departure, in this paper, I investigate how three teachers teaching a linguistically and culturally mixed fourth-grade class in a mainstream Athens primary school initiate shifts to play frames during WCI as well as how they respond to instances of pupil-initiated frame shifting to play. In particular, drawing on insights from interactional sociolinguistics, conversation analysis and ethnography, I explore these frame shifts to play by examining the 'contextualization cues' (Gumperz, 1982) the teachers use to construct play frames as well as the types of pupil and teacher uptakes they elicit.

Through such frame shifts, I argue that the three teachers make strategic uses of shifts to play as a resource, especially in assessments and sequences of reproach, and illustrate that, while tolerating pupil-led shifts to play, the teachers in question routinely avoid actively participating in such talk. In the concluding discussion, I address how, through such shifts to play, teachers and pupils do 'identity work' in the classroom. For this purpose, I adopt a social constructivist approach to identity that views the teachers and pupils' social identity construction as a dynamic process that is situated in talk-in-interaction and constituted through daily exchanges across different settings at school (Norton, 2000).

Participants, setting and data

The three teachers in this paper are the fourth grade form teacher, the English language teacher and the teacher for the class history project.[2] The fourth grade pupils form a linguistically and culturally mixed peer group that is comprised of six Greek-speaking monolinguals and five Greek-Turkish bilinguals who attend a mainstream primary school that is located in an inner-city neighbourhood in Athens, Greece.[3] The members of this class share a long history of daily interactions at school, spanning over a period of approximately four years (see Lytra, 2003, for a discussion).

The data presented in this paper are part of a larger pool of data, approximately 30 hours of tape-recorded interactions, which I collected during a four-month fieldwork in the school in question (January-May, 1998) for my PhD thesis.[4] For this purpose, I recorded exchanges among the fourth graders, their teachers and myself (the researcher) across different settings at school. To contextualize the tape-recordings, I did participant observations, informal discussions and semi-structured qualitative interviews with the participants.

Constructing play frames: teachers as initiators and respondents to play

Following Goffman (1974), frames are regarded as mechanisms through which participants structure their social and personal experiences (1974: 10-11). To interpret the intended frame, participants employ clusters of cues to signal how a given utterance, movement or gesture is to be interpreted. These 'con-textualization cues' function as framing devices and associate what is said to assumed background knowledge among participants (Gumperz, 1982: 131). To construct play frames in particular, participants send cues to each other with the message 'this is play' (Bateson, 1972: 179). On their part, participants need to have a certain degree of meta-communicative awareness in order to differentiate between those cues used for play and those employed for combat, as they tend to overlap (Bateson, 1972; also Straehle, 1993).

Overall, frames are seen as interactively constructed and emergent entities that are heavily context-dependent. Therefore, frames can be juxtaposed against, leak into or be in conflict with other frames. Moreover, interactants can shift from one frame to another or they can juggle multiple frames at the same time (Tannen & Wallet [1987]; 1993). These characteristics of frames make them a flexible tool to examine the emergence and development of play frames during WCI.

In general, the data indicate that teachers tolerate pupil-led shifts to play during WCI, thereby making play frames an enduring feature of classroom talk. Not only do pupils direct such shifts to play to fellow peers they also direct them to teachers. For instance, in excerpt 1 below, the teacher for the class history project and the pupils have been talking about the issue of the freedom of speech in fifth century Athenian democracy when she addresses a 'known-information question' (Mehan, 1985) to the whole class (line 1). Giannis makes a bid for the classroom floor, by raising his index finger and calling the teacher (line

2). Besides competing for next speakership rights, Giannis' summons also generates a reframing of the activity to play.

Excerpt 1 [5]

(Participants: Teacher; Giannis: Greek-speaking monolingual boy; Tuncay: Greek-Turkish bilingual boy)

	1	Teacher	*f* in a <u>democracy</u> . can every <u>man</u> speak <u>freely</u>?=
→	2	Giannis	=*ff* ((with sing-song intonation)) <u>Mi</u>::ss .
	3	Tuncay	*p* <u>Mi</u>::ss .
	4	Teacher	=Costa?

By exploiting loudness, stress, vowel elongation and sing-song intonation, Giannis reframes the interaction. Although the reframing does not alter the activity greatly (it is still a summons), it does attract a playful uptake by another pupil (Tuncay, line 3). This means that the summons is perceived differently (i.e. it is seen as an attempt for play), especially since it differs from the summons pupils usually employ to compete for the interactional floor: calling the teacher by making use of successive 'Miss' in fast pace, while quickly swaying their index finger. On her part, the teacher ignores Giannis' playful summons and allocates next speakership rights to Costa (another pupil who was bidding quietly for the interactional floor) instead.

When teachers occasionally initiate or participate in the construction of play frames, however, their contributions are limited to single turns. These may take the form of either an initiation or a response to a playful turn (such as a tease, a joke etc.). While such teacher talk may in turn elicit a playful uptake on the part of the pupils, including sustained laughter and giggling, teachers consistently avoid maintaining the play frame (e.g. by responding to pupil uptakes playfully). Rather, they introduce shifts to the instructional frame at hand (e.g. lesson, class management or task-related frame).

Although pupils introduce the overwhelming majority of frame shifts to play during WCI (e.g. excerpt 1 above), teachers occasionally take up the position of the initiator. For instance, in excerpt 2 below, the English language teacher is pursuing her explanation regarding the absence of plural case-marking in adjectives in English, by giving incorrect examples (i.e. talls, smalls, in lines 1, 3). She sums up her exemplification by assessing such mistakes (adding plural case-marking in adjectives) as 'very silly' ones (line 5).

Excerpt 2

(Participants: Teacher; Husein: Greek-Turkish bilingual boy; Tuncay: Greek-Turkish bilingual boy; Costas: Greek-speaking monolingual boy; Vasia: Greek-speaking monolingual girl)

	1	Teacher	*f* I can't add s to an adjective . and say .. <u>talls</u>
	2	Husein	((tries to repeat what the teacher said)) tols .
	3	Teacher	or- .. <u>smalls</u> .
	4	Husein	((tries to repeat what the teacher said)) choichs
→	5	Teacher	what would that be? .. .. [it would be a <u>very silly</u> mistake
	6	Costas	[Vasia ..
	7	Tuncay	(hh)Vasia(hh) .. (hh)made-=
	8	Husein	=*f* a <u>very silly</u> mistake
	9	( )	hhhh
	10	Teacher	*f* <u>right</u> .
	11	Tuncay	*f* a <u>silly</u> mistake
	12	Teacher	<u>therefore</u> Tuncay .. I can't add s . to an adjective .

By making use of the mild term of jocular abuse 'silly', the teacher is trying to precipitate possible mistakes pupils might make in English. Simultaneously, the use of this particular cue reframes the activity to play. Although the reframing does not change greatly the activity (it is still an assessment), it does change the pupils' perception of what is going on. As the following turns illustrate, the English language teacher's assessment triggers playful uptakes on the pupils' part (cf. Baynham, 1996): Tuncay, Costas and Husein, collaboratively engage in cross-sex teasing targeting Vasia. From their teases, it transpires that Vasia had made the mistake the teacher has just assessed as a 'very silly' one (lines 6–8).

Exchanges, such as excerpt 2 above, illustrate that teacher-led shifts to play provide opportunities for pupils to play a more active role in negotiating the main frame in classroom discourse: pupils maintain the play frame, by repeating the cues teachers have used in their talk (such as mild terms of jocular abuse) against a backdrop of teacher-led reframings to the instructional frame. Through such playful uptakes, pupils construct themselves as active participants who attempt to influence topic and frame development and control locally the on-going interaction (cf. Candela, 1999).

It is worth noting that such pupil uptakes highlight the possible hazards of teacher-initiated play frames in WCI: cues invoking informal talk among peers that teachers employ may trigger and sustain play frames over a number of turns, impeding their trailing off and the subsequent resumption of the instructional frame. As a result, to bring the play frame to a close, teachers need to initiate repeated shifts to the instructional frame, by using discourse markers and summoning a 'named addressee' (usually one of the pupils sustaining the play frame) (MacBeth, 1991: 297). For instance, in excerpt 2 above, the English language teacher makes two attempts to bring the play frame to a halt: by using the discourse markers 'so' (line 10) and 'therefore' (line 12) and resuming the point she was making before the introduction of the play frame. As excerpt 2 demonstrates, however, pupils may temporarily resist such teacher-led reframings to instruction, by opting to sustain the play frame (e.g. Tuncay's loud and emphatic repetition of the mild term of verbal abuse the teacher had used in line 11).

Besides shifts to play in assessments, teachers employ shifts to play in sequences of reproach. In general, sequences of reproach are regarded as an enduring feature of classroom life, regardless of teachers' efforts to contain them and minimise their (potentially) disruptive effect on classroom order (MacBeth, 1990: 192). In the data, sequences of reproach are frequently triggered by pupil-led shifts to play (e.g. teasing, joking). In response, teachers build their reproaches by making use of mock threats, such as 'x' (corresponding to the name of a pupil) 'you're in for a good smacking'.

A case in point is excerpt 3 below. In this excerpt, the form teacher has called Nontas to come to the blackboard to do a maths exercise. As Nontas hesitates, the teacher summons him once again to the blackboard (line 1). Following the teacher's summons, Tuncay and Costas playfully summon Nontas, by chanting his name (lines 2–3). In the next turn, Nontas elaborates on his unwillingness to come to the blackboard by quietly explaining that he does not know how to do the exercise. The teacher addresses Nontas' anxieties before she turns her attention to Costas who had produced the first and most vocal playful summons in the previous turns (line 2).

Excerpt 3

(Participants: Teacher; Costas: Greek-speaking monolingual boy; Nontas: Greek-speaking monolingual boy; Tuncay: Greek-Turkish bilingual boy)

	1	Teacher	*f* co::me on Nonta
	2	Costas	*f* No::-nta .
	3	Tuncay	*p* No::-nta .
	4	Nontas	*pp* acc I don't know how to do it ((the exercise)) .
→	5	Teacher	*acc* come ((to the blackboard)) . and I'll show you
	6		*f* Costa you're in for a goo::d smacking
	7	( )	hhh hh

Building on the playful delivery of Costas' summons, the form teacher produces a mock threat ('Costa you're in for a goo::d smacking', line 5) with the similar sing-song intonation that the two boys (Costas and Tuncay) had employed in their playful summons directed at Nontas ('<u>No::-nta</u>', lines 2–3). The teacher's contribution triggers laughter on the pupils' part, as Nontas takes his place at the blackboard to do the maths exercise and the instructional frame is about to be resumed.

It is worth noting that such mock threats are a common feature of teacher talk in the data. In her study on Greek verbal play among adults and children, Hirschon (1992) characterises mock threats as: 'statements of intention that specify some kind of violent sanction upon a tiny offender but that are seldom carried out' (1992: 39). The frequency with which adults employ such threats towards children, Hirschon argues, points to: 'a considerably greater degree of freedom to dissociate words from actions, that there is a lack of account-ability for verbal utterances, and that this applies to many more contexts than is admissible in standard English' (1992: 38–39).

In this respect, the dissociation between words and actions in Greek discourse means that these mock threats are seen as ritual threats: teachers never physically punish the pupil to whom they direct their threats and pupils know that they will never be physically punished. Rather, teacher-initiated ritual threats should be seen as a culture-specific aspect of Greek verbal discourse. Indeed, mock threats in this discourse context may function as attempts on the teachers' part to mitigate their disciplinary remarks vis-à-vis pupils' (minor) conversational transgressions (e.g. in excerpt 3 above, this conversational transgression has to do with the production of the playful summons which may have the effect of further inhibiting an already reluctant pupil from coming to the blackboard to do the maths exercise) (cf. Sifianou, 1992).

Besides being triggered by preceding play frames, as in the case of excerpt 3, teacher-initiated sequences of reproach may also generate subsequent play frames. Through the repetition of the teachers' disciplinary remarks, pupils exploit these play frames in order to lend a hand in the management of class-room discipline (Rampton, 1999). On these occasions, while, as a rule, teachers resist contributing to the development of play frames in sequences of reproach and foreground the instructional frame instead, sometimes they may collude with the pupils and momentarily revert to playfulness.

For instance, in excerpt 4 below, the teacher for the class history project and the pupils have been talking about the issue of the freedom of speech in fifth century Athenian democracy. Vasia who has had the floor prior to excerpt 4 has been consistently mispronouncing the word 'people' ('anthropoi' in Greek) by putting the stress on the second rather than the first syllable. When Giannis and Tuncay draw her attention to this mistake (lines 1, 4) Vasia snaps back at them saying that this is the way she wants to pronounce the word (lines 5). Her snapping back at Giannis and Tuncay elicits the teacher's disciplinary remarks (line 6): interestingly, the teacher does not focus on her prior utterance but rather on the fact that she is not sitting properly (she is sitting in a cross-legged position).

Excerpt 4

(Participants: Teacher; Giannis: Greek-speaking monolingual boy; Vasia: Greek-speaking monolingual girl; Tuncay: Greek-Turkish bilingual boy; Maria: Greek-speaking monolingual girl; Husein: Greek-Turkish bilingual boy)

```
      1   Giannis    f Vasia . ((it's)) the people
      2   Teacher    so . [m:::
      3   Vasia            [acc hold on a minute Gianni
      4   Tuncay     ff ((it's)) the people .
      5   Vasia      ((she shifts into a cross-legged position)) acc well I say people I do=
      6   Teacher    =Vasia . sit properly please=
      7   Maria      =acc sit properly Vasia=
      8   Giannis    =acc sit  [properly Vasia
      9   Tuncay              [acc sit   [properly Vasia
  →  10   Teacher                        [f you too Mr Husein .  [put your bottom
     11   Vasia                                                 [ hhh Mr Husein
  →  12   Teacher    [properly on the chair
     13   Vasia      [hhhh
     14   Giannis    your (hh)bottom ..
     15   Teacher    I don't want to hear ((any more of this)) Gianni
     16   Husein     your (hh) bottom .
     17   Tuncay     hhhhh
     18   Teacher    f so . in ancient Athens ..
```

Latching on the teacher's reproach, in the next turn, Maria reproduces the former's remarks ('sit properly Vasia', line 7), by making use of syntactic repetition with a minor alteration of the mode of delivery (notably, through accelerated speech) (cf. Tannock, 1999). Her contribution triggers a frame shift in talk from the teacher's serious reproach to teasing, while simultaneously appearing to contribute to Vasia's disciplining and policing classroom conduct. Following Maria's lead, Giannis and Tuncay repeat the teacher's remarks in fast pace, thereby corroborating in sustaining the play frame (lines 8–9).

In the next turns, instead of calling Maria, Giannis and Tuncay to order and shifting gear to a serious reproach, the teacher momentarily seems to be colluding with the pupils in maintaining the play frame: although she shifts the target of the reproach to Husein, her disciplinary remarks are designed in such a way that they are bound to attract more teasing on the pupils' part. In particular, she teasingly addresses Husein as 'Mr Husein' and asks him to 'put his bottom properly on his chair' (i.e. to sit properly rather than crossing his legs and leaning on his desk) (lines 10, 12). Not surprisingly, the teacher's playful disciplinary remark attracts more pupil uptakes: Vasia repeats the term of address the teacher used ('Mr Husein') and laughs (lines 11), while Giannis and Husein repeat the teacher's reference to the latter's bottom which they seem to find amusing (lines 14, 16), as attested to by their giggling and Tuncay's subsequent laughter (line 17).

Consistent with teacher contributions to play frames in WCI, subsequent to her playful reproach of Husein, the teacher makes a swift shift back to non-play: in line 15, she appears to be chastising Giannis for teasing Husein and then in line 18 she re-introduces the instructional frame that had been put on hold. Indeed, all four excerpts discussed in this paper indicate that while tolerating the initiation and development of play frames in WCI, teachers routinely avoid actively participating in sustaining them over a single turn. Instead, they ignore such contributions (e.g. excerpts 1, 2), provide minimal responses (e.g. excerpts 3, 4) and most commonly initiate frame shifts to the instructional frame (e.g. excerpts 1, 2, 4).

Concluding discussion

This study indicates that teachers consider play frames as the exception rather than the norm in WCI. This is corroborated by the fact that play frames which teachers initiate and in which they participate are strategically used as a resource mainly on specific occasions, namely in assessments and in sequences of reproach (cf. Baynham, 1996). This means that in these discourse contexts teachers temporarily foreground a legitimate, albeit limited, role for play in the centre of classroom discourse (see Lytra, 2003, for further discussion).

Regarding the cues teachers' exploit to construct play frames, the data illustrate that teachers often employ cues which invoke either informal talk among peers (excerpt 2) or mother/care giver-child interactions (excerpts 3–4). On their part, pupils perceive such cues as incongruent with classroom discourse in general and teacher talk preceding these cues in particular (see also Cook, 2000; Eggins & Slade, 1997; Hirst, 2003). This incongruence triggers subsequent pupil uptakes and provides pupils with the conversational arena to vie with teachers for local control over talk in the centre of classroom discourse.

Besides taking part in negotiations over frame and topic development, frame shifts to play give teachers and pupils the opportunity to do 'identity work' in the classroom and build social relations (Baynham, 1996; Hirst 2003; see also Maybin 2003; Rampton, 1995; 1999). While still concerned with disciplining or providing assessments, through shifts to play, teachers are also seen as enhancing their inter-personal relations with their pupils: by appropriating and introducing the 'voices' of a fellow peer or a mother/care giver, they project non-institutional social personas with which their pupils can readily identify. Nevertheless, while foregrounding such non-institutional social personas, teachers are still orientating to their teacher identities and roles. By virtue of the latter, teachers initiate sequences of reproach and use ritual threats in classroom talk. Moreover, they attempt to control topic and frame management and dictate the duration of play frames, by avoiding to construct play frames beyond a single turn and by shifting to instructional frames instead.

On the pupils' part, by resisting teacher-led reframings to instruction and maintaining the play frame (excerpt 2) or by lending a hand in the management of classroom order and transforming teacher-led serious reproaches to teasing (excerpt 4), they are enhancing their institutional or 'pupil' identities and constructing themselves as active participants in classroom talk (cf. Candela, 1999; also Davis, 1983). It is worth noting that on these occasions the pupils' diverse linguistic and cultural backgrounds seem to recede as they collude against their teachers to participate in sequences of reproach (which invariably results in generating more disorder) or they engage in cross-sex or same-sex teasing aiming at a fellow peer. In this respect, pupils appear to be foregrounding an alternative interactional order or 'counter-script' than that put forth by their teachers based on alternative and competing discourses and positionings (cf. Gutiérrez et al., 1999; Hirst, 2003). This interactional order resembles more the school playground and dining hall than the classroom and gives pupils the opportunity to bring to the fore other (non-institutional) social identities, such as identities associated with gender and peer group relations and ties (see Lytra, 2003, for further discussion).

Acknowledgements

I would like to thank members of the audience at BAAL 2003 for raising useful points regarding the data analysis as well as Janet Maybin for insightful comments on earlier drafts. The financial assistance of the Arts and Humanities Research Board and the Saripolos Foundation (University of Athens) for my doctoral studies is also greatly acknowledged.

Transcription conventions

(( ))	transcriber's comments
[	overlapping speech
. (…)	pause(s)
h(hh)	laughter
=	latching
-	marks abrupt cutting off of sound
f	spoken loudly
ff	spoken very loudly
p	spoken softly
:(:::)	lengthened vowel sound
<u>underline</u>	emphatic stress; acc spoken quickly
italics	English

References

Bateson, G. (1972) *Steps to an Ecology of the Mind.* Chicago: University of Chicago.

Baynham, M. (1996) Humour as an interpersonal resource in adult numeracy classrooms. In S. Sarangi and M. Baynham (eds) Discursive construction of educational identities: alternative readings (special issue). *Language and Education* 10(2 and 3): 187–200

Candela, A. (1999) Students' power in classroom discourse. *Linguistics and Education* 10(2): 139–63.

Cook, G. (2000) *Language Play, Language Learning.* Oxford: Oxford University Press.

Davis, B. (1983) The role pupils play in the social construction of classroom order. *British Journal of Sociology of Education* 4(1): 55– 69.

Eggins, S. and Slade, D. (1997) *Analysing Casual Conversation.* London: Cassell.

Gumperz, J. J. (1982) *Discourse Strategies.* Cambridge: Cambridge University Press.

Gutiérrez, K. D., Baquedano-López, P. and Tejeda, C. (1999) Rethinking diversity: hybridity and hybrid language practices in the third space. *Mind, Culture and Activity.* 6(4): 286–303.

Haworth, A. (1999) Bakhtin in the classroom: what constitutes a dialogic text? Some lessons from small group instruction. *Language and Education* 13(2): 99–117.

Hirschon R. (1992) Greek adults' verbal play or How to train for caution. *Journal of Modern Greek Studies* 10(1): 35–56.

Hirst, E. (2003) Diverse voices in a second language classroom: burlesque, parody and mimicry. *Language and Education* 17(3): 174–91.

Kambarelis, G. (2001) Producing heteroglossic classroom (micro) cultures through hybrid discourse practice. *Linguistics and Education* 12(1): 85–125.

MacBeth, D. H. (1990) Classroom order as practical action: the making and the unmaking of a quiet reproach. *British Journal of Sociology of Education* 1(2): 189–214.

MacBeth, D. H. (1991) Teacher authority as practical action. *Linguistics and Education* 3: 281–313.

Maybin, J. (1994) Children's voices: talk, knowledge and identity. In D. Graddol et al. (eds) *Researching Language and Literacy in Social Contexts.* 131–49. Clevedon: Multilingual Matters in association with The Open University.

Maybin, J. (2003) Voices, intertextuality and induction in schooling. In S. Goodman et al. (eds) *Language, Literacy and Education: a reader.* London: Trentham.

Mehan, H. (1985) The structure of classroom discourse. In T. A. van Dijk (ed.) *Handbook of Discourse Analysis.* Vol. 3. 119–31. London: Academic Press.

Norton, B. (2000) *Identity and Language Learning. Gender, Ethnicity and Educational Change.* Harlow, England: Longman.

Lantolf, J. P. (1997) The function of language play in the acquisition of L2 Spanish. In A. Pérez-Leroux and W. R. Glass (eds) *Contemporary Perspectives on the Acquisition of Spanish.* 3–24. Somerville, MA: Cascadilla Press.

Lytra, V. (2003) Constructing play frames and social identities: the case of a linguistically and culturally mixed peer group in an Athenian primary school. Unpublished PhD thesis, King's College, University of London.

Rampton, B. (1995) *Crossing: Language and Ethnicity among Adolescents.* London: Longman.

Rampton, B. (1999) Deutsch in inner London and the animation of an instructed foreign language. *Journal of Sociolinguistics* 3(4): 480–504.

Sifianou, M. (1992) *Politeness Phenomena in England and Greece.* Oxford: Clarendon Press.

Straehle, C. A. (1993) "Samuel?" "Yes, Dear?" Teasing and conversational rapport. In D. Tannen (ed.) *Framing in Discourse.* 210–30. NY: Oxford University Press.

Sullivan, P. (2000) Playfulness as mediation in communicative language teaching in a Vietnamese classroom. In J. P. Lantolf (ed.) *Sociocultural Theory and Second Language Learning.* 115–31. Oxford: Oxford University Press.

Tannen, D. (1986) *That's not what I Meant: how conversational style makes or breaks your relations with others.* London: J. M. Dent and Sons.

Tannen, D. and Wallat, S. ([1987]1993) Interactive frames and knowledge schemas in interaction: examples from a medical examination/interview. In D. Tannen (ed.) *Framing in Discourse.* 57–76. NY: Oxford University Press.

Tannock, S. (1999) Working with insults: discourse and difference in an inner-city youth organization. *Discourse and Society* 10(3): 317–50.

10 English in Africa and the emergence of Afro-Saxons: globalization or marginalization?

Casmir M. Rubagumya

University of Dar es Salaam

Abstract

English in Africa has recently almost become synonymous with globalization. The value of English in Africa in the era of globalization is so high that some middle-class parents are now trying to create an environment for their children to acquire English as their 'mother-tongue'. Professor Ali Mazrui has coined the term 'Afro-Saxons' to describe this emerging class of Africans whose first language is English. This paper explores the role of English and 'Afro-Saxons' in Africa today in the process of globalization. Is English and the emergence of 'Afro-Saxons' a good thing for Africa? Can English help Africa become an equal partner in the process of globalization, or is it likely to alienate Afro-Saxons from their people and marginalize the majority of African people even further? Given the current social, economic and sociolinguistic environment obtaining in many African countries, is English likely to achieve the desired objectives? The paper will focus on Tanzania in trying to understand this complex issue, although some examples will be drawn from other African countries as well.

Who speaks English in Africa?

Several scholars have argued that English belongs to all the people who use it. For the proponents of this view, individuals and communities choose to acquire a new language because it is in their interest to do so. They also argue that English cannot be said to belong to Britain or the USA (for example), and therefore the question of these two countries imposing 'their' language on other people does not arise. English, it is contended, is a world language, which belongs to everybody who uses it. This paradigm is discussed extensively by Brutt-Griffler (2002: 23) in her book *World English*. She argues:

> Language spread and change cannot be conceived through conceptual frameworks that involve historically active agents imposing their language on passive recipients. It is, rather, a process in which the essential actor is the acquiring speech community. In developing an understanding of World English, macro acquisition conceives the speech community as bringing about language spread and change.

I must say that my understanding of the spread of English in Africa is quite different from what is argued above. I think there are certain facts that are not contested:

1. European languages were *imposed* on Africa during the colonial period. African people as communities did not *choose* to learn those languages. How else can we explain why for example, Senegal is 'Francophone', Tanzania 'Anglophone' and Mozambique 'Lusophone'? Whether this imposition was a good thing or not is beside the point.

2. Individual Africans do not necessarily *choose* to learn these languages. Since the language of instruction in almost all African countries is the language of the former colonial power, going to school does not leave any choice to individual students as to which language they would like to use. By going to school, one is forced by circumstances to learn English or French or Portuguese. One might, of course, say cynically that those who don't want to learn European languages should not go to school. This leads me to the third fact.

3. Individuals who do not go to school, and therefore do not learn European languages, do not choose not to go to school. They do not have access to schooling. In Africa today the majority of the people are in this category, and educated people are a tiny minority.

So, saying that English came to Africa by choice – whether of communities or individuals, is to distort history. It might be the case that later this imposed language was seen as beneficial and therefore people continued to use it for the purposes for which it was not originally intended. This, however, does not negate the fact of an imposed colonial language. One might ask: why didn't African countries abandon English at independence if it was a language imposed by colonial rule? The answer is: it was in the interest of the ruling class in Africa to retain English after independence because of the advantages that it afforded them. English (French, Portuguese) gave the elite access to the 'fruits of independence'; access which was denied to the majority of the people in African countries. Myers-Scotton (1993: 148) has called this phenomenon elite closure. Elite closure, according to Myers-Scotton, occurs when 'the elite successfully employ official language policies and their own non-formalized language usage patterns to limit access of non-elite groups to political position and socioeconomic advancement'. Also, neo-colonial relations often militate against making decisions that may be perceived as unfriendly to former colonial rulers. For example, when Tanzania asked Britain for assistance in improving the teaching of English in secondary schools, that assistance was given, but on condition that English continued to be the medium of instruction at secondary level of education (Criper & Dodd, 1984).

In Africa today, English is used by a minority. In Tanzania, for instance, only about 5 per cent of the population has some competence in English (and levels of competence vary greatly). Elsewhere in Africa, where English is a second language, the percentage is between 10 and 20 (Schmied, 1991). Countries like South Africa and Liberia, which have substantial numbers of native-speakers of English, probably have slightly higher percentages. So, how does macro-acquisition (i.e. second language acquisition by speech communities) make sense for the African situation? What kind of communities are we talking about? Brutt-Griffler (2002) argues that English is no longer the language of the elite, that the world's English-using population has reached two billion and that it would be hard to claim the existence of two billion members of the world's elite. But in a footnote to this denial of English being the language of the elite, Brutt-Griffler (2002: 125) says, 'just as socioeconomic status at one time determined access to English, it now often governs the level of proficiency in English ultimately attained – *the highest levels [being] generally found in the social elite*' (my italics). So, English is not the language of the elite, but it is the elite who are proficient in English. Even assuming that the figure of two billion English users is correct (a debatable contention according to Graddol, 1997), how many of these are in Africa? Some speakers of English in Africa have been termed Afro-Saxons by Prof. Ali Mazrui, and it is to these that we now turn.

Who are the Afro-Saxons?

Mazrui and Mazrui (1998: 137) have suggested that in 'many parts of Africa.... there is a growing tendency for highly educated parents to use English in the home to communicate with each other as well as with their children'. Such children, who grow up speaking English as their first language, are the ones referred to as Afro-Saxons. Mazrui and Mazrui (1998) argue that Afro-Saxons are likely to emerge in African families, where (a) English is used for all or almost all communication needs, and (b) where English is a *lingua franca* of the home, especially in mixed marriages in which English is the only common language of the couple.

The phenomenon of Afro-Saxons as defined by Mazrui and Mazrui (1998) has been observed in several African countries. In Kenya, for example, it has been observed that middle-class parents raise their children in an English-speaking environment (Bunyi, 2001). These children grow up with English as their 'mother-tongue', although their parents learnt English as their second language. This group of children should be distinguished from children of white English speaking parents in countries like South Africa, Zimbabwe and Namibia. The latter group I would call African Anglo-Saxons. Similarly, Graddol (1997) has pointed out that in many developing countries, including those in Africa, there is a tendency for professional and middle-class families to adopt English as the language of the home, in which case children from these homes have no other language apart from English. They thus become Afro-Saxons *par excellence*.

In a country like Tanzania, the emergence of Afro-Saxons is hampered by the sociolinguistic environment. There are very few Tanzanian couples for whom English is the only language of communication. For the majority, Kiswahili is the language of the home. There are, however, some parents who try to create an artificial environment at home by forcing their children to use English. These efforts are usually not successful because the playground is a Kiswahili speaking domain. The main motivation for these parents to want their children to become English speakers, it is often argued, is because English is essential in today's globalized world.

What does globalization mean for Africa?

Ask anybody in Africa why they need English, and the answer will invariably be 'because of globalization'. But if you ask what globalization is, and how English will help them in the globalization process, the answer is not as straight forward. I want to try and understand what globalization means for Africa, and in the process see if English is a *sine qua non* of Africa being integrated in the so-called global village. The first observation to make is that even if we accept the logic of the global village, this is a village where there are a few chiefs – very powerful economically and militarily – and a lot of powerless villagers. The global village is therefore characterized by unequal power relations, and I will try to show that English is an integral part of these relations, not a solution to them.

Chachage (2001) argues that globalization is an era when consumer dominance is the new logic of society and not real societal needs. Individuals are integrated into this consumer society through seduction or repression. It is an era marked by the supermarket ideology 'which goes as far as defining love in terms of the relationship between a person and his/her car, revolution as a new brand of soap, and freedom as possession of a cellular phone'. One could add that it is this market ideology which has given birth to the term 'globalization' and abolished the term 'imperialism'. The market has indeed replaced imperial armies, but one wonders whether the effect is any different.

How then, are Africans affected by this new ideology and what is the role of English in it? I will try to give some examples from Tanzania, but I believe similar examples can be found all over Africa. First, globalization means market forces: opening national markets for global competition. In Tanzania today, supermarkets are full of fruit juice from South Africa. Yet Tanzania produces a lot of fruits. Most of these rot because there is no market for them, and farmers are discouraged because they cannot get a good income from their labour.

So how can English help a small farmer in Tanzania benefit from this kind of globalization? Only business people who import fruit juice from South Africa can benefit. Most often these are owners of supermarket chains, which are subsidiaries of supermarkets in South Africa.

Second, globalization means opening national boundaries for Foreign Direct Investment (FDI). Here again I will give an example of how South Africa has penetrated the Tanzanian market. I am sure most of you have heard of Tanzanite, a gemstone found only in Tanzania. Before the liberalization of the economy, Tanzanite was mined by small-scale miners in cooperatives. More recently, a South African company called Afgem has been given license to mine Tanzanite. As soon as they started business, they said that all Tanzanite stones on the world market must bear the Afgem imprint. What this means is that they now have the monopoly of the Tanzanite business, and the small-scale miners can do nothing about it. It is interesting to note that the chairperson of Afgem (Tanzania) Board of Directors is the former Tanzanian Ambassador to South Africa. I want to suggest that for Mr. Ambassador, English is an important asset which has given him a niche in the globalized Tanzanite business. For the small-scale miners, whether they know English or not is irrelevant. Globalization for them means loss of a livelihood.

Third, globalization means the privatization of parastatal companies formerly owned either fully or partially by the government. Once these companies are privatized, new owners – whether foreign or nationals – drastically reduce the work force, ostensibly for efficiency. In many parts of Africa, this has thrown many people out of work. (This is euphemistically called downsizing or making the privatized company slim.) Here again, it is doubtful whether

English is of much use to the thousands of people who have lost their jobs due to privatization.

Fourth, globalization means the government drastically reducing spending on social services like health and education. The outcome of this is again opening these services to the logic of market forces: only those with enough income can enjoy them. In the education sector, it means that only children of relatively well-off parents have access to quality education, including quality English language education. The rest will go through the motions of learning English – and there are unscrupulous people who will cash on this market – but at the end of the day the English learnt is dismal.

Can English help Africa to benefit from globalization?

Given what globalization means for Africa, what can English do to help Africans integrate into the globalized economy? The economy of Africa is marginalized. For example, of the 500 largest global corporations, not even a single one is in Africa (Graddol, 1997). I would like to suggest that if Africa is not playing a significant role in the world economy, English will not help her to do so. In fact economic marginalization makes the learning of English very difficult because of lack of adequate resources. It seems to me then, that those who argue that English will help us to go global miss the point. It is by being part of the global economy – by producing competitive goods and services – that we can learn English effectively. It is therefore not the case that more English will lead to African global integration; the reverse is more likely.

So far, English has failed to help Africans get the requisite knowledge, skills and capital needed for effective competition in the world market. The reason for this is not very difficult to see. Knowledge, as defined by the school system in African countries, is accessible by only a minority of African people in a language not understood by the majority. As Prah (2003) correctly argues, the language of schooling in any country is also the language of hegemony and power. It is the language in which basic skills and knowledge are imparted to the population, and the medium in which knowledge is produced and reproduced. Since in Africa education is in European languages, which the majority of the people have no access to, the implication is that they are denied this knowledge, while traditional knowledge, which they have access to in their languages, is devalued. Secondly, even the few who have access to schooling are disadvantaged because the language of instruction is an impediment to getting knowledge. Roy-Campbell (2001: 17) makes more or less the same point when she contends:

> As education makes available to the populace the culture, language,

knowledge and skills needed for the society to reproduce itself and produce new forms of knowledge, schools, which are social and historical constructs, are important sites for the formal reproduction of that knowledge... Those who do not acquire the requisite cultural capital are disadvantaged in accessing the resources distributed and opportunities available for full participation in the society.

Globalization will elude Africa unless we start with the basics. Recently a colleague from Mozambique was telling me that HIV/AIDS in his country cannot be contained because campaigns against HIV/AIDS are in Portuguese, a language the majority of the people do not understand. I am sure this kind of mistake is made in many African countries. If we have no survival strategies, in a language understood by our people, who will see the day to be part of the global community?

The emergence of Afro-Saxons will only make Africa more dependent on the west. Afro-Saxons can only be agents of western multinational corporations. Globalization and liberalization have not created a viable middle-class in Africa, with enough capital to compete in the global markets. The middle-class in Africa is therefore insignificant: consumers rather than producers, dependent rather than dynamic, so unlikely to sustain itself. Real economic power for Africa will come from regional integration *a la* European Union. This kind of integration, if it is to involve the majority of the people (i.e. not only the elite) will make sense in languages like Kiswahili, Hausa, Wolof, Lingala, Zulu etc.

As Graddol (1997: 44) rightly argues:

> Regionalization may encourage the use of a non-English *lingua franca* for trading purposes. Greater use of Spanish in South America, for example, may affect the popularity of English in Brazil, just as interest in learning English in Hong Kong has recently been affected by the perceived priority of Mandarin.

Likewise, greater economic activity within African regional trading blocks (e.g. East African Community, SADC, ECOWAS etc.) is likely to be meaningful in regional African languages, not in English, French or Portuguese.

Implications for the ELT profession in Africa

Giving false hopes that everybody can have access to 'World English' is unethical. It helps neither the learners of English nor the language itself. I will try to illustrate my point by briefly describing the use of English language in Tanzanian English-medium primary (EMP) schools (Rubagumya, 2003). In

Tanzania, Kiswahili is the medium of instruction in public primary schools (7- to 14-year old children). At secondary and tertiary levels, the medium of instruction changes from Kiswahili to English. However, in recent years there is a tendency by middle-class parents to send their children to private, English-medium primary schools. These parents send their children to English-medium primary schools mainly for the English language; concerns about the quality of education (e.g. teachers, materials, the curriculum etc.) take second place in the parents' priorities. In fact for some parents English language is synonymous with quality education. Those who establish EMP schools are motivated by the urge to provide a needed service to the community (because public provision of education is inadequate), an 'appetite' by parents for EMP schools, and the possibility of earning an income. While it is true that some EMP schools are providing a needed service, others are unfortunately taking advantage of parents' demand for English to make money, and in the process they short-change the parents. This is the kind of opportunism being referred to by Ayo Bamgbose (2001) in the ELT profession.

The majority of teachers in EMP schools have more or less the same qualifications as their colleagues in Kiswahili-medium primary schools. Their English language proficiency is grossly inadequate. To expect them to teach effectively through the medium of English is unrealistic, to say the least.

Globalization is of course often cited as one of the reasons why parents send their children to EMP schools. I have already argued above that I do not believe English will help Africa to become an equal partner in the global community. EMP schools, as they exist today, are certainly not in a position to achieve this. What we see is the language of schooling increasingly becoming a segregating factor in society. Elite children attend private EMP schools while children of common people go to public, Kiswahili-medium primary schools. What this means is that in Tanzania education is becoming a commodity to which only those with financial power can have access. As Chachage (2001: 3) rightly argues, this is an era when it is said it is possible for the state to withdraw from the social provisioning since the market can fill the vacuum created by this withdrawal. EMP schools in Tanzania have to be understood in this context. Even within this 'open' market for education, wider educational objectives are sacrificed at the altar of English. Parents don't ask whether their children know maths, science, geography, etc. but whether they can speak English. Quality education is confused with English proficiency, and because of this confusion and the reality on the ground (incompetent teachers, inadequate teaching materials, etc.), children often end up getting neither in a satisfactory way.

It needs to be stated of course that this elitist tendency in educational provision is not peculiar to Tanzania. Almost throughout the world education tends to reproduce the ruling class. It is something, in the words of a colleague of mine, 'mysterious which is accessible to only a select few under rigorous conditions, like a secret society of witches' (Rugemalira, personal communication). Meerkotter (2003: 35) expresses the same view of education when he argues that 'schools have a tendency in a market economy to maintain the socio-economic stratification of the population and could even work against the ideal of a stable democracy capable of ensuring safe, secure, prosperous and peaceful living spaces for all citizens'. Proponents of this elitist view of education will argue that the value of education is maintained only if it remains the preserve of a tiny minority.

Let me say emphatically that I am not against the learning of English in Tanzania in particular, and Africa in general. English is a very useful language and people should be encouraged to learn it. However, learning English should not be at the expense of indigenous African languages, nor should it be at the expense of getting meaningful education. The learning of English should be premised on *additive*, as opposed to *subtractive*, bilingual policy. Mejia (2002: 40) describes additive bilingualism thus:

> Additive bilingualism refers, on the one hand, to the positive cognitive outcomes which result from being bilingual on an individual level, and on the other, to the enrichment of language, culture and ethnolinguistic identity at a societal level. In these cases, an individual acquires or learns a second or foreign language without detracting from the maintenance and development of his or her first language. The second or foreign language is seen as 'adding to' and enriching language experience, rather than replacing the first language.

The problem in Africa is that learning English (also French and Portuguese) is conceived in terms of subtractive bilingualism, whereby English is over-valued while African languages are under-valued. The aim is often replacing African languages by English, although this aim is rarely successful. Given the present globalization euphoria, it will take strong political will to put in place policies and practices in favour of African languages. Today, South Africa with its policy of 11 official languages (i.e. English, Afrikaans and nine indigenous African languages) is a model to be emulated by other African countries. However, one has to add that South Africa is a model for *policy*, not for *practice*. As Chick (2002: 470) clearly shows:

> Despite multilingualism being the official policy, English only discourse is pervasive and enjoys institutional support at local level. English is

presented as a unifying force; as a vehicle of economic advancement and as the appropriate choice in prestigious domains such as the classroom. By contrast, Zulu (and other African languages) are presented as a potentially divisive force.

We see here then, that policy and practice are not congruent. Nevertheless, a progressive policy is a step in the right direction.

Conclusion

In this paper, I have tried to show that despite claims to the contrary, English is by and large still an elite language in Africa. I have also argued that English is unlikely to help Africa integrate into the 'global village'. On the contrary, policies pursued in the name of globalization, including the valuing of English at the expense of African languages, are likely to marginalize the majority of African people. This is not an argument *against* English, it is an argument *for* the valorization of African languages. If we want sustainable development in Africa, it should be based on our rich indigenous knowledge and culture, and self-respect. English should be seen as an additional language, which will allow Africans to communicate with other people and learn from them. As Bgoya (2001: 291) rightly points out:

> Globalization is here and (it) is not going away, and there are really two responses to it: to accept its inherent anti-people logic and to succumb to its power, or to understand it, and to decide consciously to strengthen the local base and its own capacities for internal generation. As far as language is concerned, the struggle must not be reduced to English versus indigenous languages; rather it should be elevated to indigenous languages plus English – or any other foreign language for that matter.

I would like to end with an appeal to all those who are, directly or indirectly, involved in teaching English to speakers of other languages. In our day to day professional activities, we should ask ourselves the following questions:

1. How is the concept 'World English' going to affect the majority of people in the world who don't speak English?

2. Teaching 'World English' is big business: who benefits from this business?

3. What are our responsibilities as teachers of English within the context of globalization?

It has been argued that teaching English to speakers of other languages need not necessarily involve cultural alienation. For example, Modiano (2001: 344) asserts:

The teaching and learning of a geographically, politically and culturally 'neutral' form of English, which is perceived as a language of wider communication and not as a possession of native speakers, is one of the few options we have at hand if we want to continue to promote English language learning while at the same time attempting to somehow 'neutralize' the impact which the spread of English has on the cultural integrity of the learner.

This, in my view, is the biggest challenge facing English language teachers in Africa and elsewhere it is taught as a second or foreign language. How can we separate English from the cultural 'packaging' that usually comes with it in form of teaching materials, teachers' world view, etc.? How can we separate the English we get on the TV set in our living room (BBC, CNN,) from the western world view embodied in it? These are difficult questions, but they need to be asked.

References

Bamgbose, A. (2001) World Englishes and Globalization. *World Englishes* 20(3): 357–63.

Bgoya, W. (2001) The effect of globalization in Africa and the choice of language in publishing. *International Review of Education* 47(3/4): 283–92.

Brutt-Griffler, J. (2002) *World English: a study of its development.* Clevedon: Multilingual Matters.

Bunyi, G. (2001) Language and educational inequality in primary classrooms in Kenya. In M. Heller and M. Martin-Jones (eds) *Voices of Authority: education and linguistic difference.* 77–100. Westport: Ablex Publishing.

Chachage, S. (2001) Mammon and Lazarus: conceptualizing democracy and activism against impoverishment. Paper presented at the Gender Studies Conference and Festival, Dar es Salaam.

Chick, J. K. (2002) Constructing a multilingual national identity: South African classrooms as sites of struggle between competing discourses. *Journal of Multilingual and Multicultural Development* 26(6): 462–78.

Criper, C. and Dodd, W. A. (1984) *Report on the Teaching of the English Language and its Use as a Medium of Education in Tanzania.* Dar es Salaam: The British Council.

Graddol, D. (1997) *The Future of English?* London: The British Council.

Mazrui, A. A. and Mazrui, A. M (1998) *The Power of Babel: language and governance in the African experience.* Chicago: University of Chicago Press.

Meerkotter, D. (2003) Markets, language in education and socio-economic stratification. In Brock-Utne, B., Z. Desai and M. Qorro (eds) *Language of Instruction in Tanzania and South Africa.* 35–44. Dar es Salaam: E&D Limited.

Mejia, A. M. (2002) *Power, Prestige and Bilingualism.* Clevedon: Multilingual Matters.

Modiano, M. (2001) Linguistic imperialism, cultural integrity and EIL. *ELT Journal* 55(4): 339–46.

Myers-Scotton, C. M. (1993) Elite closure as a powerful language strategy: the African case. *International Journal of the Sociology of Language* 103: 149–63.

Prah, K. K. (2003) Going native: language of instruction for education, development and African emancipation. In Brock-Utne, B. Z. Desai and M. Qorro (eds) *Language of Instruction in Tanzania and South Africa.* 14–34. Dar es Salaam: E&D Limited.

Roy-Campbell, Z. M. (2001) *Empowerment through Language.* Trenton: Africa World Press Inc.

Rubagumya, C. M. (2003) English medium primary schools in Tanzania: a changing 'linguistic market' in education. Unpublished Research Report, University of Dar es Salaam

Schmied, J. J. (1991) *English in Africa: an introduction.* London: Longman.

11 Creativity, conformity, and complexity in academic writing: tensions at the interface

Mary Scott and Joan Turner

Institute of Education and Goldsmith's College

Abstract

The perspective developed in this paper lies at the interface between applied linguistic research on academic writing and the various theoretical discourses that feed into academic literacy or academic literacies. We look at excerpts from student texts and how they enact heteroglossia, by, among other things, negotiating contemporary disciplinary discourses which the students are working on, inter-relating academic conventions such as citation with previous educational values, and developing an argument. These texts throw up questions around academic conventions, and hence academic writing pedagogy. On the one hand, they cannot be ignored, but on the other hand, the aim should be to provide understandings not rules.

Academic literacy and its discourses

The field of academic literacy or academic literacies has received a considerable amount of attention from educators, applied linguists, and others of late, and hence the field has been revitalised. Theoretical perspectives feeding into the area include social practice perspectives on academic writing (e.g. Ivanic, 1998; Lea & Street, 1998; 1999; Jones, Turner & Street, 1999; Lillis, 2001; Lillis & Turner, 2001); the implications for academic writing of the social construction of knowledge (e.g. Bazermann, 1988; Myers, 1990; Geisler, 1994; Berkenkotter & Huckin, 1995; Hyland, 2000); pedagogical approaches to academic writing (e.g. Belcher & Braine, 1995; Johns, 1997; Zamel & Spack, 1998; Lea & Stierer, 2000). Such multiplicity of input into a field, however, adds to its complexity. Different perspectives are foregrounded in one context, excluded in another, while at the same time, multiple overlappings occur.

One influential perspective comes from an enhanced understanding of 'Discourse' (to borrow Gee's [1990] convention of referencing Foucault's approach) which sees language use as enacting, and hence perpetuating, pre-existing cultural models. Such models are often those dominant in a culture or society and their dominance exerts the kind of hegemonic power which excludes other cultural models. Much of the work done in 'new literacy studies' (e.g. Gee, 1990; Street, 1995) is concerned with opening up spaces of resistance to such dominance. Issues of power and perpetuation on the one hand therefore, and how far, and in what contexts resistance is possible, on the other are major concerns of literacy in education and other social contexts. In the academic context, for example, one debate has waged around issues of pragmatism in EAP. While Benesch (1993; 2001) sees EAP teaching as overly 'accommodationist' to normative institutional requirements, seeking to induct students uncritically into academic life, Allison (1996: 85) critiques her and Pennycook's (1994) 'reductive' position that pragmatism represents 'a unified discourse offering constant ideological support to an unexamined educational, academic and sociopolitical status quo.' In a rejoinder to what he saw as Allison's 'defence of pragmatism' Pennycook (1997) elaborated a distinction between 'vulgar' and 'critical' pragmatism, along the way critiquing the 'discourses of neutrality' which made a position of 'vulgar pragmatism' readily available in EAP.

The site of tension, which this debate has created, comes sharply into focus when working with an individual student's writing. On the one hand, the teacher wants to help the student achieve the best from their academic endeavours, which usually means accommodating to institutional norms for academic literacy. On the other hand, the teacher wants to foster critical language awareness (cf. Fairclough, 1992) and help students project their own voice in their writing, whilst at the same time positioning themselves within their disciplinary discourses (see further in examples discussed below). The complexity of these issues is often undermined in institutional discourse around language however, where academic literacy is simply 'common sense' (cf. Lillis, 1999). At the level of institutional discourse, expectations of academic literacy tend to be normative, embodying 'the modern consciousness' whose values the Scollons (1981) associated with what they called 'essay-text literacy'. Essay-text literacy is associated with a distant, disembodied voice, as projected by a prototypical European Enlightenment scientist 'discovering' knowledge and making it visible (cf. Turner, 2003). Such an objectivist relationship to knowledge has of course been challenged in many areas of the social sciences and humanities, but its rhetorical effects continue to hold sway in the conventions of academic writing. Academic literacy then, is an unstable arena of competing assumptions and expectations, where there is some room for rhetorical innovation but also deeply entrenched norms around institutional practices of assessment and evaluation. These norms in English demand textual cohesion, which includes making logical relationships explicit as well as grammatical accuracy and nuance in lexical choice.

Mediating academic literacy

In this section, we are looking at examples of work from L2 students and the issues of mediation that arise. The function of mediating academic literacy is often called 'language support' but drawing on Baynham's (1995) use of 'literacy mediators', we prefer to talk of mediating academic literacy. This does not mean that we write for the student, but attempt to mediate between the background assumptions the student is working with and the dominant institutional assumptions that will make the work acceptable, as well as help the student mediate between the disciplinary discourses s/he is working with and positioning her/himself within them.

The following student is working in the area of visual culture, and drawing on the theoretical discourses of postcolonialism and psychoanalysis. She is extremely competent and well versed in those discourses, able to explain or expound at length, orally, on any question asked. However, as the following extract illustrates, the issue of grammatical and lexical accuracy in English, as well as deictic coherence throughout the excerpt get in the way of reader accessibility.

> In other words, I discuss the 'voice-symptomatic' (un)consciousness with which the sexual slave women spoke in South Korea during the 1990s which appears in the site of contestation within/beyond the 'ideological' consciousness and the state of knowledge determined by the ideologically organized normative discursive performative relations between Japan and Korea and its postwar political and economical relations.

Reading heteroglossia

Recognizing that all texts are the products of heteroglossia (Bakhtin, 1981), i.e. of competing voices, the question we would ask of the paragraph above is: What is the nature of this text's heteroglossia? This is a question that can reconfigure the student's 'problem with English' especially if it is linked to a view of academic writing as a creative act in which the student writer consciously or intuitively seeks to reconcile the competing voices that beset her.

These voices may be numerous; for example, the voices of past instruction; the voices of current tutors; the loud or faint voices of the student's assumptions and expectations regarding writing in English or the demands of a particular course. (Scott, 2001; 2002). However, in this paper we focus on the echoes of the student's reading in her text, paying particular attention to the heteroglossic tensions that shape it.

The student is researching repressed voices in Korea that are struggling to be heard, i.e. the voices of the 'other'. Her research involves her in reading texts about otherness by authors who create a 'style' or 'voice' that seeks to capture 'otherness'. These writers may demonstrate the conventional features of academic writing (e.g. nominalisation or the passive voice) but they use the features in a particular way. The following example is from De Certeau's (1986: 3 & 4) history of psychoanalysis, an essay that the student had consulted:

> History is 'cannibalistic', and memory becomes the closed arena of conflict between two contradictory operations: forgetting, which is not something passive, a loss, but an action directed against the past; and the mnemic trace, the return of what was forgotten, in other words, an action by a past that is now forced to disguise itself. More generally speaking, any autonomous order is founded upon what it eliminates; it produces a 'residue' condemned to be forgotten. But what was excluded infiltrates the place of its origin – now the present's 'clean' [*propre*] place. It resurfaces, it troubles, it turns the present's feeling of being 'at home' into an illusion, it lurks – this 'wild', this 'ob-scene', this 'filth', this 'resistance' of 'superstition' within the walls of the residence, and, behind the back of the other (the *ego*), or over its objections, it inscribes there the law of the other.

As is typical of this kind of writing, De Certeau packs the abstractions with ambiguities and paradoxes [*an order founded on what it eliminates*]; he crosses boundaries or creates in-between spaces in metaphors that juxtapose abstraction and the concrete; (*closed arena of conflict*; *action...disguise*; *behind the back of the other*); he invents terms ('*cannibalistic*'); uses punctuation in unconventional ways (a comma before *in other words*; a hyphen in *ob-scene*), and he favours the series as a syntactical means of intensifying meaning (e.g. a series of verbs or adjectives or nouns or elaborative and appositional clauses as in *it surfaces resurfaces, it troubles, it turns; this 'wild', this 'ob-scene', this 'filth', this 'resistance' of 'superstition'*). Generally speaking, this way of writing – this style – enacts 'otherness' largely by means of syntactical features associated with spoken English (e.g. the co-ordinating conjunctions, *and, but*; the placing of pauses, e.g. before *But*; the parentheses, the juxtaposition of phrases; the use of punctuation to direct the reading). This close-to-speech style conforms to psychoanalysis, the talking cure, in its attempt to capture resonances that evade the rationality of conventional academic argument. It is to this voice, which challenges the conventions of scientific writing, that the text largely owes its readability.

Turning again to the student's text we note that there are echoes of the voices of the authors she is reading. This might be said to be appropriate in view of the fact that her subject is otherness; the return of the repressed. But the student's text represents a problematic hybrid. She is caught between the voice that is required in PhD writing and the voices she encounters in her reading. Her opening sentence (*In other words I discuss*) represents a conformity to the PhD requirement that the writer's purposes be made explicit. The student has also sought explicitness in her syntactically problematic attempt to weld together the different content components of what she wants to say (*with which...*; *which...*). On the other hand, the voices of her reading are clearly discernible in *voice symptomatic*; in the list of pre-head noun qualifiers – *organized normative discursive performative relations*; and in the slash to suggest ambiguity: *within/beyond*.

We would suggest that the student's perceived problem with language as illustrated in this passage, is rooted in her twofold 'otherness', i.e. in the space she occupies in between the expectation that she write for an 'intelligent outsider' – to quote advice frequently given to doctoral students – and make her purposes clear, and the style of the texts she is reading, which, for all their complexity of content are readable. The student's text is not; she has created a mosaic – a visual construct in which there is little sense of a writer's voice. To express the problem another way by borrowing Bakhtin's (1981) terms, the centripetal voice of the PhD clashes with centrifugal echoes of the texts she has read.

Doctoral students who are doing research that requires a substantial amount of reading inevitably 'pick up' features of the texts they read. We would now argue strongly that academic literacy tutors and subject tutors need to give attention to helping students to understand the larger issues relating to knowledge-making that are reflected in the style of texts from their field of study. The aim should be to provide students with understandings not rules – understandings of how and why the texts they read and the texts they are expected to produce are as they are. Students should then be in a position to exploit the creative potential of heteroglossic tensions such as those we have illustrated above.

What we are suggesting gives 'language' a context that is very different from the institutional discourses referred to earlier. However, while the student's text is undoubtedly problematic as we have indicated, a question remains. How should students write about topics in fields of knowledge that challenge the view of rationality on which the PhD is largely based? How postmodern might a PhD thesis be? The conventions of academic writing have, of course, been challenged, especially by feminist researchers but the focus has tended to be on the explicit inclusion of personal experience and feelings as in the example below which comes from a PhD thesis:

> Teachers setting homework would request us to 'look this up in the encyclopaedia when you get home'. Not only did this mean I was unable to do the homework, I was constantly constructed as 'other' and inferior, for coming from a home where these and other resources were not readily available. Casual mentions of ski-ing holidays in Switzerland and days out to places of interest in London and elsewhere re-inscribed this sense of outsiderness, and made me long for (and know that I could not have) what looked like a life of excitement beside which mine seemed increasingly tedious and dull.

This view of the importance of the personal in knowledge-making certainly represents a challenge to a view of rationality that is held to express itself in impersonal sentence constructions but it is a long way from postmodern ways of writing which seek to capture resonances in a style that is more usually associated with the poetic or with Deleuze and Guattari's (1994) view of literary style as affect divorced from propositional meaning. In this paper we can only use our example to suggest that there are more questions to be asked about writing and knowledge-making in different fields of study than have yet been addressed.

Widening the focus

The tensions around language in academic writing do not occur only at the doctoral level, however. The question we have asked – What is the nature of this text's heteroglossia? – is relevant at all levels of higher education. The examples that we have selected to make this point are from an assignment by a student on an in-service degree course in Education. The student trained as a teacher in a country where, for economic reasons, training colleges did not have well-stocked libraries. This influenced the modes of teaching and learning and made it impossible for lecturers to set assignments that would require the critical reading of a number of texts.

The student's draft of her first written assignment was seen as demonstrating a 'problem with writing in English'. In her written feedback to the student the tutor made the following numbered comments

1. You need to write in full sentences.

2. Referencing needs care. Consult the course handbook for examples of how to set out references in the body of a text.

Each instance of these problems was underlined and the appropriate number – 1 or 2 – was written in the margin of the student's assignment.

The following are three examples of the kinds of sentence that were identified as problematic. Each represents a recurring problem in the student's text.

> (Dave, 1975) Explain that lifelong education represents the inner necessity of men to continually exceed themselves

> Preparation for life in tomorrow's world cannot be satisfied by a once and for all acquisition of knowledge and know-how. By John Field (2001),

> According to the Secretary of State for Education and Employment he wrote that 'To cope with the rapid change and the challenge of the information and communication age, we must ensure that people can return to learning throughout their lives'.

We acknowledge the need for the student to become familiar with ways of integrating citation into text, and of referencing sources but we would argue that the examples above have a larger significance. As in the case of the PhD student, we read the student's writing as evidence of the student's struggle to reconcile competing voices. The discourses about academic writing that the student has been offered on her course are relevant to our interpretations. The student has been told in seminars that an essential feature of academic writing is an 'argument' in which the writer develops her own position – her own voice – in relation to the relevant literature of the field. She has also been advised to acknowledge her sources. These are requirements which Baynham (1999), drawing on Bakhtin, succinctly describes as 'double-voicing in the construction of a scholarly 'I'.

The examples quoted above demonstrate the student's attempt to meet these requirements. However, the student's style of referencing can also be read as articulating her uneasiness regarding the requirement that she position herself in relation to the voices of the 'others' that she has encountered in her reading. As we indicate below, a closer look at the examples reveals an interesting pattern. In each case the student has constructed a hierarchy by visually and syntactically marking out a space in which her voice and that of the other to whom she refers are both joined and disjoined.

In the first example the student places the subject of the sentence, Dave, in brackets. She then inserts a phrase of her own: *Explain that.* The use of the capital 'E' and of the plural form in *Explain* can be read as mere technical errors. However, we would suggest that they should rather be viewed as the student's intuitive attempt to indicate that the direct quotation of Dave's words which follows – *lifelong education represents the inner necessity...* – do in fact signify a position that is shared by her and Dave. The absence of quotation marks is in keeping with this interpretation. It is not an equal sharing, though. The student's placing of Dave, with date, in brackets at the beginning of the sentence gives his name greater prominence than the conventions of integral referencing would allow. In visually setting Dave apart from herself the student endows Dave, the other, with superior status in the particular field of knowledge-making.

In the second example the student attributes the status of an authority to the cited author by giving him a space of his own that is pegged out by an emphatic, initial *By* and the use of both his first and family names: *John Field.* Interestingly there are no examples of conventional non-integral referencing in the student's assignment. In each case where that would be appropriate she uses the 'By' construction. It is as if she needs to emphasise that the quotation she has just used to build her argument comes from someone whose authority transcends hers.

The third example demonstrates a pattern that is frequently encountered in L2 students' academic writing, viz., the anaphoric use of a subject pronoun with verb after 'according to...'. (*According to..., he wrote...*). However, this instance suggests that it may be relevant to consider who is being quoted. Here the student's syntactically unacceptable use of *he* gives emphasis to the authority of the Secretary of State – the kind of authority which the student said was very highly respected in her country of origin. The Secretary of State's voice of authority is further accentuated by the student's enclosure of his words in quotation marks, a device she did not use in the first two examples above. In thus creating a space between her voice as referee and the voice of the State's representative the student signals the power of the State. It clearly has a voice that needs to be heeded.

Like the PhD student whose writing was discussed earlier, this student occupies an in-between space. In her case it is a space between an institutional past and an institutional present with their different requirements. However, what the examples from this student's writing also indicate is the operation of desire at the centre of student writing. This is almost certainly the case with all writing but it may be more salient when the student is an L2 writer from an educational context with different expectations of student writers from those that characterise higher education in the UK. The student is anxious to meet the referencing requirements but for her this is not merely a technical issue. Desire conflicts with attitudes and feelings towards the 'other' in the form of the voices in the books she reads – voices that she endows with authority. In fact it might be said that the processes that postmodern writers like De Certeau knowingly try to capture in their writing are being unwittingly demonstrated by student writers like the two whose writing we have considered in this paper.

We acknowledge that our readings of the student's texts are open to question as is always the case with interpretations. We hope, however, that we have stimulated reflection and debate. The writer in the text is currently the focus of a substantial amount of research that looks at 'evaluation' or 'stance'. For example, Hunston and Thompson, (2000); Hyland, (2000); Charles, (2003). This research is based on the analysis of large corpora which are compiled almost exclusively from the publications of professional academic writers. Illuminating though such studies are, they tend to suggest a transmission mode of pedagogy with students being taught linguistic patterns that characterise social interactions in the knowledge-making of different disciplines. Such a pedagogy cannot accommodate the complexities of individual histories and socially shaped 'structures of feeling' (Williams, 1977) in student encounters with new educational contexts. On the basis of the discussion above we would argue that it is here that pedagogy needs to begin.

References

Allison, D. (1996) Pragmatist discourse and English for academic purposes. *English for Specific Purposes* 15(2): 85–103.

Bakhtin, M. M. (1981) *The Dialogic Imagination: four essays*. [Edited by M. Holquist; translated by C. Emerson and M. Holquist.] Austin: University of Texas.

Baynham, M. (1995) *Literacy Practices. Investigating Literacy in Social Contexts*. London and New York: Longman.

Baynham, M. (1999) Double-voicing and the scholarly 'I'. On incorporating the words of others in academic discourse. *TEXT* 19(4): 485–504.

Belcher, D. and Braine, G. (1995) (eds) *Academic Writing in a Second Language. Essays on Research and Pedagogy*. Norwood, NJ: Ablex.

Benesch, S. (1993) ESL, ideology, and the politics of pragmatism. *TESOL Quarterly* 27: 705–17.

Benesch, S. (2001) *Critical English for Academic Purposes. Theory, Politics, and Practice*. Mahwah, NJ: Lawrence Erlbaum Associates.

Charles, M. (2003) This mystery – a corpus-based study of the use of nouns to construct stance in theses from two contrasting disciplines, *Journal of English for Academic Purposes* 2(4):313–26.

De Certeau, M. (1986) *Heterologies: discourses on the other.* [Translated by
    B. Massumi.] Minneapolis and London: University of Minnesota Press.
Deleuze, G and Guattari, F. (1994) *What is Philosophy.* [Translated by
    H.Tomlinson and G. Burchill.] London: Verso.
Fairclough, N. (1992) (ed.) *Critical Language Awareness.* London:
    Longman.
Gee, J. P. (1990) *Social Linguistics and Literacies: ideology in discourses.*
    London, New York, Philadelphia: Falmer Press.
Geisler, C. (1994) *Academic Literacy and the Nature of Expertise.* Hillsdale,
    NJ: Lawrence Erlbaum Associates.
Hunston, S. and Thompson, G. (2000) (eds) *Evaluation in Text: authorial
    stance and the construction of discourse.* Oxford: Oxford University
    Press.
Hyland, K. (2000) *Disciplinary Discourses. Social Interactions in Academic
    Writing.* Harlow England, London, New York, etc.: Pearson Education.
Ivanic, R. (1998) *Writing and Identity. The Discoursal Construction of
    Identity in Academic Writing.* Amsterdam: John Benjamins.
Johns, A. (1997) *Text, Role, and Context. Developing Academic Literacies.*
    Cambridge: Cambridge University Press.
Jones, C., Turner, J. and Street, B. (1999) (eds) *Students Writing in the
    University:cultural and epistemological issues.* Amsterdam and
    Philadelphia: John Benjamins.
Lea, M. and Street, B. (1998) Student writing and staff feedback in higher
    education: an academic literacies approach. *Studies in Higher Education*
    23(2): 157–72
Lea, M. and Street, B. (1999) Writing as academic literacies: understanding
    textual practices in higher education. In C. N. Candlin and K. Hyland
    (eds) *Writing: texts, processes and practices.* 62–81. London and New
    York: Longman.
Lea, M. R. and Stierer, B. (2000) (eds) *Student Writing in Higher Education:
    new contexts.* Buckingham; Philadelphia, Pa: Open University Press.
Lillis, T. (1999) Whose 'Common Sense'? Essayist literacy and the insti-
    tutional practice of mystery. In C. Jones, J. Turner and B. Street (eds)
    Students Writing in the University: cultural and epistemological issues.
    127–47. Amsterdam: John Benjamins.
Lillis, T. and Turner, J. (2001) Student writing in higher education: contem-
    porary confusion, traditional concerns. *Teaching in Higher Education*
    6(1): 57–68.
Myers, G. (1990) *Writing Biology: texts in the social construction of scien-
    tific knowledge.* Madison, WI: University of Wisconsin Press.

Pennycook, A. (1994) Incommensurable Discourses? *Applied Linguistics* 15(2): 115–38

Pennycook, A. (1997) Vulgar pragmatism, critical pragmatism, and EAP. *English for Specific Purposes* 16(4): 253–69.

Scott, M. (2001) Written English, word processors and meaning making. In L. Tolchinsky (ed.) *Developmental Aspects of Learning to Write.* Dordrecht: Kluwer Academic Publishers.

Scott, M. (2002) Cracking the codes anew: writing about literature in England. In D. Foster and D. Russell (eds) *Writing and Learning in Cross-National Perspective: transitions from secondary to higher education.* Urbana: NCTE and Mahwah, NJ: Lawrence Erlbaum Associates.

Street, B. (1995) *Social Literacies.* London: Longman.

Turner, J. (2003) Academic literacy in post-colonial times: hegemonic norms and transcultural possibilities. *Language and Intercultural Communication* 3(3): 187–97.

Williams, R. (1977) *Marxism and Literature.* Oxford: Oxford University Press.

Zamel, V. and Spack, R. (eds) (1998) *Negotiating Academic Literacies. Teaching and Learning Across Languages and Cultures.* Mahwah, New Jersey: Lawrence Erlbaum Associates.

12   A Cantonese syllabary for English soccer

Geoff P. Smith

University of Hong Kong

Abstract

Representing English names in oral and written Chinese is a challenge because of significant differences between the phonologies of the two languages. This is exemplified by problems faced by commentators in Hong Kong who need to find suitable names for teams and players in reporting the highly popular English Premier League soccer matches. Inspection of the names used shows that most are phonetic equivalents, although in a number of cases, translation of semantic elements is attempted. While phonetic representations predominate, they can be problematic. The lack of fit between the two sound systems may make for poor equivalence, and the written characters invariably have meanings of their own, which may provide an unwelcome intrusion.

English soccer in Hong Kong

The English Premier League teams have many supporters in Hong Kong, rather more than those who support local teams. The large glamorous clubs such as Manchester United, Arsenal and Chelsea attract the most attention, and for some, declaring support for one of these teams can be seen as something of a fashion statement. However, there are large numbers of genuine soccer aficionados, both local and expatriate, and those who have access to cable TV have a wide range of Premier League matches to choose from. These are typically broadcast live and complete on Saturday and Sunday evenings (Hong Kong time) and repeated several times over the next few days. Generally, the live broadcasts are accompanied by commentaries from English-based experts, but on the Chinese-language channels, a live commentary in Cantonese, the main language of Hong Kong, is superimposed. In the interval, panels of experts in matching coloured blazers discuss the progress of the game in Cantonese. Team lists are sometimes given in English, but sometimes also or exclusively in Chinese characters. Names of teams are by now well known, and usually given exclusively in Cantonese during discussion in Chinese.

English and Cantonese phonologies compared

Rendering English names in Chinese always represents something of a challenge. English and Cantonese are genetically and typologically far removed from each other. While English belongs to the Indo-European family, Cantonese is a member of the Sino-Tibetan group. As might be expected, there are a number of significant differences between the phonologies of the two languages, which makes representing the sounds of one in those of the other potentially difficult. First of all, Cantonese is a tonal language. The number of tones described varies according to different authorities, and according to whether the so-called clipped tones (really unreleased stops) are included. Excluding these, there are seven tones which can be distinguished in Cantonese, but due to the effective merger of high level and high falling tones, only six different lexically significant pitch contours are distinguished in the contemporary Hong Kong variety (Bauer, 1998). English has a somewhat larger phoneme inventory, with a significantly greater number of vowels and although there is a considerable overlap in the broad nature of some of the consonants, English has a much greater number of fricatives: eight, compared with two in Cantonese. Moreover, Cantonese syllable structure imposes constraints not found in English; consonant clusters are not allowed, and syllables consist minimally of a vowel, with an optional initial consonant and final nasal or unreleased stop (Matthews & Yip, 1994). Within this general framework, certain combinations of initial and final consonant are not permitted, for example, a syllable may not begin and end with a labial consonant (Bauer & Benedict, 1997). Representing English words in Cantonese phonology can therefore be a problem, especially where exotic fricatives and consonant clusters are involved. This is illustrated below by the way some English team names are represented in Chinese characters according to Cantonese pronunciation.

Representing Premier League teams

The following is a chart of the Premier League teams in the 2002–3 season plus the three teams which were promoted to the current season's league. The English name in the first column is represented by written Chinese characters in the second column and its pronunciation in Cantonese is given in the third columns according to the Yale Romanisation. This system uses 'h' after vowels to represent the three low tones with diacritic marks (acute and grave accents) to represent rising and falling contours. Thus, the tones of the syllables *maahn lyùhn* representing Manchester United are low level and low falling respectively.

Team	Chinese	Cantonese pronunciation
Manchester United	曼聯	maahn <u>lyùhn</u>
Arsenal	阿仙奴	a sìn nòuh
Newcastle	紐卡素	náu kà sou
Chelsea	車路士	chè louh sih
Liverpool	利物浦	leih maht póu
Blackburn	布力般	bou lihk bún
Everton	愛華頓	(ng)oi wàh deuhn
Southampton	修咸頓	sàu hàahm deuhn
Manchester City	曼城	maahn <u>sìhng</u>
Tottenham Hotspur	熱刺	yiht chi
Middlesboro	米杜士堡	máih douh sih bóu
Charlton	查爾頓	chàh yíh deuhn
Birmingham	伯明翰	baak mìhng hohn
Fulham	富咸	fu hàahm
Leeds	列斯聯	liht sì <u>lyùhn</u>
Aston Villa	阿士東維拉	a sih dùng wàih làai
Bolton	保頓	bóu deuhn
West Ham	韋斯咸	wàih sì hàahm
West Brom	西布朗	<u>sài</u> bou lóhng
Sunderland	新特蘭	sàn dahk làahn
Portsmouth	樸茨茅夫	pok chìh màauh fùh
Wolverhampton	狼隊	lòhng deuih
Leicester	李斯特城	léih sì dahk sìhng

A direct translation of the Chinese terms is not given here for all the teams, as most of the meanings are irrelevant, and the Chinese equivalent is merely based on the sound of the English name subject to the constraints of Cantonese phonology. Those teams with sounds represented by phonemes similar in the two languages will be relatively transparent, for example, *chè louh sih* 'Chelsea' and *a sìn nouh* 'Arsenal'. Conversely, sounds not common to the two phonologies will present problems, and the resemblance of the Cantonese versions of these names may not be so obvious to English speakers. For example, the consonant clusters and exotic phonemes in 'Portsmouth' are represented by the rather unwieldy combination *pok chìh màauh fùh*.

Only the meaning of those teams that actually include a semantic element will be described here. The syllables representing semantic translations are underlined in the table above. The first two are 城 (*sìhng*) and 聯 (*lyùhn*) to represent two commonly appended names throughout the football leagues: 'city' and 'united' respectively. Thus Manchester United is 曼 聯 *maahn lyùhn* while Manchester City is 曼 城 *maahn sìhng*. Other Premier League teams using these titles are Leeds United 列 斯 聯 *liht sì lyùhn* and Leicester City 李 斯 特 城 *léih sì dahk sìhng*. That leaves only two teams with names represented semantically, Tottenham Hotspur and Wolverhampton Wanderers. Tottenham is named 熱 刺 *yiht chi* which literally means 'hot thorn or spike'. The expression 馬 刺 *máh chi* 'horse spike' refers to a spur used by horsemen, and the title is thus a translation of Tottenham's 'Hotspur' nickname, commonly reduced to 'Spurs'. Similarly, Wolverhampton Wanderers are predictably nicknames 'Wolves'' and the team's name in Chinese is 狼 隊 *lòhng deuih* meaning 'wolf pack'. No other team on this list is represented by a semantic translation in Hong Kong, although on one Premier League website based in Mainland China, Southampton is represented by 南 安 普 頓 – *nan2 an1 pu3 dun4* in Mandarin (Putonghua) pronunciation (the numbers represent tones) – where the first character means 'south'.

Semantic elements in other team names

Looking through the team names of other English divisions, the situation is largely similar – most are phonetic representations of the English names. Only a handful of teams employ semantic elements in their translations as detailed below:

Team	Chinese	Cantonese Pronunciation
Crystal Palace	水 晶 宮	séui jìng gùng
Nottingham Forest	諾 定 咸 森 林	nohk dihng hàahm sàm làhm
Sheffield Wednesday	錫 周 三	sèk jàu sàam
Sheffield United	錫 菲 聯	sèk fèi lyùhn
Derby County	打 比 郡	dá béi gwahn
Queens Park Rangers	昆 士 柏 流 浪	gwàn sih paak làuh lohng
Blackpool	黑 池	hàk chìh
Oxford	牛 津	ngàuh jèun
Cambridge	劍 橋	gim kìuh
Arsenal (previously)	兵 工 廠	bìng gùng chóng

The name for Crystal Palace is a direct translation: 水 晶 *séui jìng* 'crystal' and 宮 *gùng* 'palace.' Nottingham Forest is split between the phonetic representation of Nottingham 諾 定 咸 *nohk dihng hàahm* and the translated meaning of 'forest' 森 林 *sàm làhm*. Sheffield's name, too, is based on the pronunciation 錫 (菲) *sèk (fèi)* while the cities two teams are distinguished semantically as 錫 菲 聯 *sèk fèi lyùhn* 錫 周 三 *sèk jàu sàam*. 聯 *lyùhn* as noted above represents 'United' while 'Wednesday' is translated as 周 三 *jàu sàam*, literally 'week three' or Wednesday. A similar combination of phonetic and semantic elements is seen in the case of the West London club Queens Park Rangers and Derby County. Queens Park is represented phonetically as 昆 士 柏 gwàn sih paak while the meaning of 流 浪 làuh lohng 'a wanderer' approximates that of 'Ranger'. (The same term is sometimes used in the full name of Blackburn Rovers). Similary, 'Derby' is represented by the phonetic equivalent 打 比 *dá béi* while 'County" is translated as 郡 *gwahn* 'county, canton, region'. Oxford and Cambridge are somewhat exceptional in that the names are famous in their own right and so already have conventional representations. Oxford is a literal semantic equivalent 牛 津 *ngàuh jèun* which combines the characters for 'cow, ox' and 'ford, river crossing'. Cambridge is a mixture of the phonetic 劍 *gim* and 橋 *kìuh*, which means 'bridge'. Only one other team, Blackpool, is represented by a semantic equivalent 黑 池 *hàk chìh* literally 'black' and 'pool'.

Problems with phonological equivalence

It is seen above that the great majority of teams are represented by phonetic equivalents in Cantonese. There may also be pressure on those few teams represented semantically to adopt phonetic forms, as it appears that formerly the team Arsenal was designated by 兵 工 廠 *bìng gùng chóng* 'munitions factory,' but is now universally referred to as 阿 仙 奴 *a sìn nouh*. There is some inconsistency, for example, 'West' in West Ham is phonetic 韋 斯 *wàih sì*, while West Bromich is represented by 西 *sài* 'west.' Those that use semantic equivalents generally translate the nicknames of the teams, as is apparently common in other sports such as basketball. Thus with the Chicago Bulls, the city is represented according to the well known phonetic equivalent 芝 加 哥 *jì gà gò* while the team nickname is 公 牛 *gùng ngàuh* 'bull.' Similarly the Detroit Pistons are the 底 特 律 *dái dahk leuht* 'Detroit' 活 塞 *wuht choi* 'piston'.

However, using phonetic equivalents is not without its problems. These are mainly of two kinds: poor sound correspondence and the intrusion of the meaning of the characters used. Firstly, as noted above, not all equivalents are transparent, depending on the fit between the English and Cantonese sounds involved. Cantonese speakers may come to know the more popular of these names while not necessarily recognising the original English name. Even those who speak English to quite a high level may have a seriously reduced phoneme inventory (Hung, 2000). This problem is not confined to team names, but for any names represented in the press. For example, I had a great deal of difficulty finding out from my Chinese-speaking colleagues the identity of an American whose name was represented in press reports as 拉 姆 斯 菲 爾 德 *làai móuh sì fèi yíh dàk*. As was eventually discovered, this was considered to be the best choice for 'Rumsfeld,' a name truly exotic to Cantonese both in phonemic content and syllable structure. English-speaking readers may like to attempt to work out the identities of the following teams or players from their Cantonese equivalents. (The answers are provided at the end)[1].

溫 布 頓	wàn bou deuhn
甘 士 比	gam sih béi
高 雲 地 利	gòu wàhn deih leih
洛 達 咸	lok daaht hàahm
普 雷 斯 頓	póu lèuih sì deuhn
基 寧 咸	gèi nìhng hàahm
舒 利 亞	syù leih a

The name of one team from a lower league proved to be highly puzzling. Crewe Alexandra was represented on one website by 克 魯 *hàk lóuh* which bears little resemblance to either word. The meaning of the characters 'restrain' and 'vulgar' also seemed to have little relevance. However, this appears to be a case where similarity to a Mandarin name has established a precedent. By feeding the character combination 克 魯 into Google, many websites containing the pair appeared in the combination 克 魯 尼 which is pronounced *ke4 lu3 ni2* in Mandarin, and is the name by which the currently popular actor George Clooney is widely known. Hence, *ke4 lu3* may have been adopted by analogy for Crewe (the 'l' being the closest equivalent to the exotic phoneme 'r'). However, this leaves the Cantonese version high and dry as the virtually unrecognisable *hàk lóuh*.

Although traditional syllabaries of Cantonese do exist, such as Feng (1962), there is nevertheless considerable variability in which character is used to represent certain sounds when finding equivalents for English names. The sounds '*si*' or '*jing*' for example, could be represented by the Cantonese pronunciation of several dozen Chinese characters. The choice partly depends on meaning considerations, but some choices appear to be fairly random where there are a large number of choices available. There is a tendency for equivalents on the mainland to represent each consonant of an English name by a separate syllable, hence the appearance of such unwieldy equivalents for player names as that for McManaman 麥 克 馬 納 曼 *mahk hàk máh naap maahn*. This rendering is sometimes seen, in spite of the fact that, ignoring tone, the more popular alternative 麥馬拿文 *mahk máh nàh màhn* is virtually identical to English. There also appears to be a preference for two syllable constructions. The name Lee (李) is very common in Hong Kong, but the player Robert Lee's name is nevertheless represented as the disyllabic 李爾 *léih yíh*. It also appears that equivalents are worked out from the written forms, as, for example, the name for Le Saux 拿索斯 *nàh sok sì* attests. A two-syllable equivalent much nearer to the actual pronunciation (/ləsəʊ/) could easily be found.

The second source of problems when dealing with sound equivalents is that every syllable used has a meaning too. A careless selection could lead to the unintentional creation of some unfortunate meanings. The ideal is to find something which has positive connotations, and preferably with a similar meaning as well, but this is obviously a difficult task. Names of countries such as 英國 *yìng gwok* 'England' (literally 'noble country') and 美國 *méih gwok* (literally 'beautiful country') follow this principle. It is also a problem which faces companies marketing names familiar from the west, the best known example probably being Coca Cola. The original attempts were apparently combinations of characters attempting to represent *ko ka ko la* in Mandarin. The meanings, although largely nonsensical, usually ended with the character 蠟 *la4*, which implied that the product was some kind of wax. Hence an alternative was found, *ke3 kou3 ke3 le4* (可口可樂), which is not quite so close to the target sound, but still recognisable, and to which a meaning approximating 'happiness in the mouth' can be attributed. However, now that this has been established, the pronunciation in Cantonese *hó háu hó lohk* is nothing like the original. In Hong Kong, I have found two examples of what appear to be fairly successful cases where sound and meaning correspondence have been effectively combined. One is for the soap product 'Opal' represented as 澳寶 *ou bóu*. This sound is quite close to the English pronunciation of opal, especially in those varieties with a final 'dark l', and the expression can be given the meaning 'Australian jewel'. The other example is the mobile phone company Smartone, represented by the similar sounding 數碼通 *sou máh tùng* which means 'digital communication.'

Problems with unintended meaning seem to have been generally avoided in Premier League team names. One possible exception is the name of the team Liverpool 利物浦 *leih maht póu*. The inclusion of *maht* as the second syllable may seem a strange equivalent for 'ver', but presumably this is due to the established name for the city in Mandarin, where 物 is pronounced *wu4*. By itself, the combination does not make any sense, but if the tones are changed, a negative meaning can be contrived from the sounds. The Cantonese expression 離譜 *lèih póu* means 'beyond the limit' usually in a negative sense. The particle 乜 *màt*, literally 'what' can be inserted in expressions such as this as a euphemism in place of obscene intensifiers, so the expression 離 乜 譜 *lèih màt póu* could be considered as something like the milder English form 'f-ing intolerable'.

Conclusion

The differing phonologies of Cantonese and English present problems not only for Cantonese speakers attempting to learn English (Chan & Li, 2000) and English speakers attempting to learn Cantonese (Li & Richards, 1995) but for translators who wish to provide credible phonetic equivalents of English names in Cantonese. The current practices in representing English soccer teams and players have limited success in finding acceptable equivalents according to the closest phonetic choice, while occasionally a semantic translation becomes established.

The problems of soccer commentators may seem rather trivial, but they do have considerable significance for other more serious issues. Chinese people attempting to master English have used the system of pronouncing characters to represent English sounds since the Chinese Pidgin English phrasebooks published in Chinese in the earlier decades of the nineteenth century. And such a system is still used today in the almanacs largely devoted to predicting events according to the traditional Chinese calendar – most have a few pages devoted to representing some common English terms in Cantonese sounds. Furthermore, decisions on the representation of brand names, geographical locations, prominent people and other terms likely to have wide currency need to take into account the varying pronunciations the possible choices will have in different varieties of Chinese, as well as other languages such as Japanese that make use of the characters.

Note

1. Wimbledon, Grimsby, Coventry, Rotherham, Preston, Gillingham, Shearer.

References

Bauer, R. S. (1998) Hong Kong Cantonese tone contours. In S. Matthews (ed.) *Studies in Cantonese Linguistics*. 1–33. Hong Kong: Linguistic Society of HK.

Bauer, R. S. and Benedict, P. K. (1997) *Modern Cantonese Phonology*. Berlin and New York: Mouton de Gruyter.

Chan, A. Y. W. and Li, D. C. S. (2000) English and Cantonese phonology in constrast: explaining Cantonese ESL learners' English pronunciation problems. *Language, Culture and Curriculum* 13(1):67–85.

Feng Si Yu (ed.) (馮思禹 編) (1962) 廣州音字彙 *Guang zhou yin zi hui (A Cantonese pronunciation syllabary)*. Hong Kong.

Hung, T. N. T. (2000) Towards a phonology of Hong Kong English. *World Englishes* 19(3): 337–56.

Li, D. C. S. and Richards, J. C. (1995) *Cantonese as a Second Language: a study of learner needs and Cantonese course books. Research Monograph No. 2.* Hong Kong: City University.

Matthews, S. and Yip, V. (1994) *Cantonese: A comprehensive grammar.* London: Routledge.

13 Motivation in foreign language learning

Marion Williams

University of Exeter

Abstract

This paper first presents the case for a multifaceted approach to motivation. A model is presented where internal learner factors and external factors influencing a learner's motivation are identified. This led to the construction of the Language Learning Motivation Questionnaire. This can be used with individuals or groups as a diagnostic tool, or as a research instrument to investigate motivation on a larger scale. The results of a study in the South West of England revealed that girls were more motivated than boys, younger learners were more motivated than older ones, and pupils were more motivated to learn German than French. The participants provided clear reasons for the gender and language differences in interviews.

Introduction

One of the striking characteristics of much of the work being carried out in the area of motivation is the narrowness of focus taken by many researchers and theorists. This is readily demonstrated, for example, in the three edited volumes by Ames and Ames (1984; 1985; 1989) in which each one of some 30 chapters represents an often radically differing perspective. Whilst in-depth investigation of one aspect of motivation such as goal theory or interest is necessary to enable us to understand better some of the primary contributors to motivated action, there are also dangers in taking too narrow a focus and drawing wide generalisations from limited data.

Williams and Burden (1997) argue that such studies could be usefully complemented by adopting a multifaceted approach to motivation, and that taking such a broad perspective could provide a constructive way to help us to understand motivation particularly as it pertains to learning in schools. Such an approach is exemplified by the work of Dörnyei (1998) and is further illustrated in the review article by Wigfield, Eccles and Rodriguez (1998).

Over the years there has been a considerable body of research into motivation to learn foreign languages. Much of this has been based on the work of Gardner and his co-workers in Canada. Gardner's view of motivation derives from a socio-educational approach to learning in which motivation is defined as effort plus desire plus favourable attitudes towards learning the language (Gardner, 1985); thus attitude has always been seen as an important construct in foreign language motivation. Gardner makes the well-known distinction between two different motivational 'orientations', integrative and instrumental. Those who are integratively oriented learn the language in order to integrate with native speakers of the language whereas those who are instrumentally oriented are learning the language in order to further other goals such as promotion at work or passing exams.

Although a considerable body of research has been based on Gardner's model, in more recent years there have been a number of criticisms of the narrowness of his focus and a call by those working the area of applied linguistics to incorporate more cognitive approaches to the subject emanating from the field of educational psychology (Dörnyei, 1994a; 1994b; Oxford, 1994; Oxford & Shearin, 1994; Crookes & Schmidt, 1991).

A motivational model relating to language learning

Drawing upon the research literature in the two disciplines of psychology and applied linguistics, it was possible to construct a model of language learning motivation with three main characteristics:

1. It emphasises the dynamic interaction of external and internal factors, as is illustrated in Figure 1.

    The main external influences are identified here as parents, teachers and peers, together with aspects of the wider social, physical and psychological environment. In taking a constructivist perspective to explaining motivated action, what becomes important is the sense that individuals make of the contribution of significant others. The sense that individuals make of the influences around them and the conceptions they have of themselves enable them to make decisions regarding their actions and behaviour. Thus decisions are in the centre of the model.

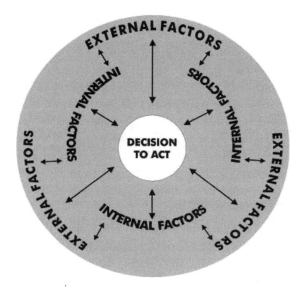

Figure 1 Interplay of external and internal factors

2. Building upon this constructivist perspective, a number of significant internal factors represented in the research literature were identified and categorised under the headings of attitudes, identity and agency, as follows:

Attitude	Identity (self-concept, self-esteem)	Agency
[What do I think about it?]	[How do I see myself?]	[How do I do it?]
to the task	sense of competence	self-efficacy
to the language	perceived ability	locus of control
to speakers of the language	self-worth	locus of causality
to learning languages	achievement motivation	motivational style
to learning	attributional style	effort
issues:		attributions
liking/interest		strategies
desire		• cognitive
challenge		• metacognitive
value		(planning, goal-setting,
• extrinsic/intrinsic		evaluation)
• instrumental/integrative		• decision making

Table 2 Categorisation of internal factors related to motivation

3. The model emphasises the importance of a person's cognitive processing of their actions as shown in Figure 2. It is a stage model beginning with the individual's construction of meaning and leading into self-regulated action.

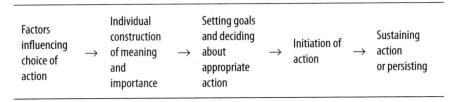

Figure 2 Cognitive processing aspects of motivation

This differs from many other models of motivation by going beyond notions of influences on action to include decisions about action and the action itself.

Questionnaire construction

Drawing upon this model it was possible to construct a questionnaire that incorporates many of the elements previously identified within the research literature. This questionnaire, referred to as the Language Learning Motivation Scale (LLMS), consists of 16 constructs, each containing four items subdivided into four areas, as shown below:

1. Attitude

   Constructs
   enjoyment and interest
   desire
   perceived importance
   integrative orientation
   intrinsic motivation

2. External influences

   Constructs
   teacher influence
   parental influence
   group ethos

3. Identity

   Constructs
   sense of competence
   perceived ability

4.   Agency

Constructs
expended effort
effort outcomes
attributional awareness
strategic awareness
sense of responsibility
metacognitive strategies

The construction of the scale is described in Williams, Burden and Lanvers (2002), where high levels of reliability for each construct, as indicated by Cronbach's alpha, are presented. Sample items are presented in Table 2.

Factor	Example
Learners' attitudes	
Enjoyment and interest	I enjoy French lessons
Desire	I want to learn to speak French well
Perceived Importance	It will be important for me to know French
Integrative orientation	I'd like to meet French people
Intrinsic motivation	I'd like to learn French even if I didn't have to
External influences	
Teacher influence	My teacher is helpful to me in learning French
Parental influence	My parents encourage me to learn French
Group ethos	The students in our class work well together as a group
Identity	
Sense of competence	I usually do well in French lessons
Perceived ability	I think I'm good at French
Agency	
Expended effort	I work hard at French
Effort outcome	However hard I try, I'll never do well in French
Attributional awareness	When I get good marks in French I usually know why
Strategic awareness	If I do badly at French, I usually know how to do better next time
Sense of responsibility	Doing well in French is up to me
Metacognitive strategies	I try to set myself goals when I study French

Table 2 Sample items

A four-point scale was used ranging from 'definitely true' to 'definitely not true'. Thus 16 was the maximum score possible and four the minimum for each of the constructs.

Questionnaire scores can then be transferred onto a Language Learning Motivational Profile (see Figure 3) which can provide a graphic portrayal of the different aspects of motivation of an individual or a group. The segments can be shaded. The first circle represents a score of four, the second eight, the third 12 and the outer circle 16.

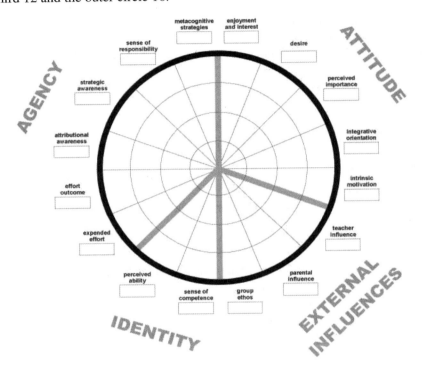

Figure 3 Language Learning Motivational Profile

Ways in which the scale can be used

The scale can be used in a number of different ways : individual, class and larger-scale use.

1. *Individual*

The scale can be used with individual students in order to obtain a profile of specific areas in which they are more or less highly motivated. The students can then be encouraged to reflect on these and to set personal goals for improvement whilst the teacher looks to ways in which s/he can contribute to boosting low areas of motivation.

2. *Group*

The scale can be used with a specific group of language learners to help the teacher to better understand the general level of motivation in his or her class. It can also be used to raise the learners' awareness of their own attitudes and motivation. After completing the questionnaire, individuals can compile their own profile by adding up their scores and entering them on the motivational profile. This could lead to a group discussion of the reasons why some constructs are seen more positively or negatively than others, and, ways in which they could work together to foster a more positive motivational climate.

3. *Larger-scale use*

The questionnaire can be used by researchers interested in investigating the motivation of language learners in a particular region, country, or cultural context. It can be used to examine general levels of motivation, differences between boy and girls, differences between groups studying different languages, differences between schools or classes, or, differences between age groups.

The study

This questionnaire was employed in an exploratory study of the motivation of secondary school students in three schools in South West of England ($n = 228$; females = 115, males = 113) to learn different foreign languages at different stages in their secondary school careers. The research questions guiding this investigation related to the general levels of motivation of the students towards learning foreign languages, the influence of specific motivational factors, the possible effects of age and gender and the likelihood of a differentiated response to the language studied (in this case French and German). The results of this study are reported in Williams, Burden & Lanvers (2002).

The overall mean scores of the sample on each motivational factor revealed a moderate to fairly high level of motivation on most dimensions, with the strongest motivational factors being an appreciation of the result of effort in learning as well as a sense of responsibility for one's own learning (mean scores 13.27 and 13.01 respectively). The weakest contribution was the influence of the learning group (mean 9.99) and the perceived use of metacognitive strategies (mean = 10.18). Neither intrinsic motivation (mean = 10.53) nor perceived importance of learning foreign languages (mean = 10.13) were particularly strong.

Table 3 shows the significant differences found between students in Year 7 (their first year in secondary school) and Year 9 (their third year). In all cases where there was a difference the younger students were found to be more highly motivated than their older peers. Particularly noteworthy here is the apparent decline in the perceived use of metacognitive strategies in learning between Year 7 and Year 9.

	Year 7 [N = 125]	Year 9 [N = 96]	Difference [7 - 9]	sig
Attitude				
perceived importance	11.14	10.17	0.96	*
integrative orientation	12.51	11.06	1.45	**
External influences				
teacher influence	13.54	12.24	1.30	**
Identity				
sense of competence	12.48	11.40	1.08	**
perceived ability	12.57	11.83	0.74	*
Agency				
expended effort	13.02	11.97	1.05	**
metacognitive strategies	11.22	8.91	2.30	**

using independent samples t-test
** $p \leq 0.01$
* $p \leq 0.05$

Table 3 Differences between Year 7 and Year 9

Table 4 shows the differences between boys and girls, and reveals a consistently higher level of motivation among girls than boys on seven of the 16 motivational factors. Of particular note here is that it is largely in their attitudes towards learning foreign languages (four out of five factors) that the girls out-score the boys, whilst in the area of agency they indicate that they are prepared to expend more effort in learning and recognise positive learning outcomes from doing so.

	Boys [N = 109]	Girls [N = 108]	Difference [G -B]	Sig
Attitude				
enjoyment and interest	10.25	11.99	1.74	**
desire	11.44	13.43	1.98	**
integrative orientation	11.05	12.71	1.67	**
intrinsic motivation	9.64	11.40	1.76	**
Agency				
expended effort	11.76	13.32	1.56	**
effort outcome	12.89	13.64	0.74	*
metacognitive strategies	9.68	10.66	0.98	*

using independent samples t-test
**$p \leq 0.01$
*$p \leq 0.05$

Table 4 Differences between boys and girls

When a comparison was made between the motivation of the sample as a whole towards learning French or German, significant differences were found on 11 of the 16 factors in favour of learning German. However, when a separate analysis was made for girls only, no significant differences were found on any motivational dimension with regard to either language. Further analysis of boys' motivation revealed a significant motivational preference for German over French on 14 dimensions. Particularly strong here was teacher influence. See Table 5.

	French [N = 53]	German [N = 59]	Difference (G - F)	Sig
Attitude				
enjoyment and interest	9.26	11.20	1.94	**
desire	10.42	12.33	1.91	**
perceived importance	9.56	11.18	1.62	*
integrative orientation	10.31	11.69	1.38	*
intrinsic motivation	8.92	10.31	1.66	**
External influences				
teacher influence	11.57	13.75	2.18	**
parental influence	9.59	12.09	2.50	**
group ethos	9.08	10.99	1.91	**
Identity				
sense of competence	10.90	12.27	1.37	*
perceived ability	10.90	12.88	1.98	**
Agency				
expended effort	11.24	12.26	1.02	n.s.
effort outcome	12.02	13.67	1.65	**
attributional awareness	10.60	12.37	1.77	**
strategic awareness	11.14	12.74	1.60	**
sense of responsibility	12.59	13.43	0.84	n.s.
metacognitive strategies	8.79	10.45	1.66	**

using independent samples t-test
** $p \leq 0.01$
* $p \leq 0.05$

Table 5 Differences between French and German for boys only

The results of the questionnaire were followed up using interviews. Both girls and boys were able to provide explanations for the gender differences. Several explained that it was not considered 'cool' for boys to show an interest in foreign languages. As a Year 7 girl commented:

'some of them might like it but they just don't want to show it'

while a Year 9 girl explained –

'it's just they don't want teasing from the other boys'.

There were however, differences between boys and girls in their attitudes towards French and German, with French being seen as a feminine sounding language. A Year 9 girl commented:

'I reckon girls are more into French, they like the way that French sounds more than boys do'

while a Year 9 boy graphically explained –

'French is meant to be the language of love and stuff [while German is] the war, Hitler, and all that.

When invited to talk about the strategies that they used to learn languages, most participants found it extremely difficult to discuss this aspect at all. This possibly reflects a general scarcity of opportunities to discuss learning strategies within our educational system. When asked if she ever decides herself what to do, a Year 9 girl replied –

'Not really. She tells us what to do and that's it really'

while a Year 9 boys said –

'It's up to the teacher what we learn and that's that, so really you have to do what they say and get on with it.'

When invited to talk about their attitudes towards learning foreign languages, the students' opinions ranged from highly positive attitudes with clearly articulated aims to distinctly apathetic ones. As one participant explained –

'I mean I need a language to actually do what I want to do, to get on with my life, but at the same time it's good to have a language just in case you need it'

and another was clear about his goals –

'I wanna be able to speak the language cause I want to go into industrial technology where you need languages'.

On the other hand there were a number of responses of the following type:

Interviewer: Do you think it's going to be important to you?
Student: Don't know.

and –

'It's just that I don't care if I can speak the language.'

Discussion and implications

It would be inappropriate to attempt to draw sweeping conclusions from this small-scale study, the results of which can only be seen as tentative and, at best, hypothesis-generating. Nevertheless, the findings do have interesting and potentially significant implications for future research and educational policy.

Firstly, the Language Learning Motivation Scale shows signs of being a robust instrument, meeting acceptable standards of validity and reliability. Moreover, it confirms the results of the review of the psychological literature in this area that motivation to learn is a multifaceted construct which needs to be approached from a broader perspective, incorporating a number of contributing factors, if its process and effects are to be properly understood. Although the 16 elements incorporated into the LLMS are not inclusive of all aspects of motivation (any reference to motivational style is a notable omission, for example), the differential pattern of responses to the different elements provided by subgroups within the sample demonstrates once again the complexity of the phenomenon of motivation. What is needed now are studies involving larger and more widely representative samples, as well as longitudinal studies to substantiate results obtained from cross-sectional samples. At the same time, structural equation modelling should help to provide further data about both the significant contribution of different variables and the connection between them.

As far as the results themselves are concerned, there are several implications for further research and intervention. The declining motivation throughout the secondary school years, as has been found in many studies e.g. Helinke (1993), Chambers (1999), needs to be explored further and challenged on a number of counts. Does it happen invariably across all individuals, schools and communities? If so, are there reasons unconnected with language learning itself or is this due to the nature of school-curriculum based subjects? Have some schools found the secret of maintaining (language learning) motivation? Is this pattern similar in other countries or communities?

When it comes to the languages to be learnt, the preferences shown in the present study are interesting. Although it is very common in the UK (and in other countries such as Australia) for French to be the first foreign language to be taught, the theoretical rationale for this is not at all clear. The results of this study would appear to indicate that, for boys at least, German might prove to be more accessible and motivating. Moreover, the results from a further study into the attributions of secondary school students for their successes and failures in learning languages (Williams & Burden, in preparation) suggests that Spanish may well be the first language of choice for English school students. These are not simple matters to unravel, but what is suggested here is that there is a need to question long-established, commonly-held assumptions about what languages to teach for whom and when.

Another finding to emerge from this study is the enormous gap in the motivation of girls and boys to learn foreign languages. This is, of course, not a new phenomenon, and the findings can be seen to replicate those of several other studies in this area (Barton, 1997; Graham & Rees, 1995; Cohen, 1998, Stables & Wikeley, 1999). The use of individual interviews to delve more deeply into the questionnaire results help to shed further light on this, as well as supporting the combination of both quantitative and qualitative methods in real-world research (Tashakkori & Teddlie, 1998).

Finally, much more research of a similar nature in the real-world settings of schools and communities is needed if the potentially helpful insights pertaining to motivation emanating from psychological theories are to be tested out in practice and eventually have the impact they deserve.

References

Ames, C. and Ames, R. E. (1984) (eds) *Research on Motivation in Education, vol. 1. Student Motivation.* London: Academic Press.

Ames, C. and Ames, R. E. (1985) (eds) *Research on Motivation in Education, vol. 2. The Classroom Millieu.* London: Academic Press.

Ames, C. and Ames, R. E. (1989) (eds) *Research on Motivation in Education, vol. 3. Goals and Cognitions.* London: Academic Press.

Barton, A. (1997) Boys' under-achievement in GCSE modern languages: reviewing the reasons. *Language Learning Journal* 16:11–16.

Chambers, G. (1999) *Motivating Language Learners.* Clevedon: Multilingual Matters.

Cohen, M. (1998) A habit of healthy idleness: boys underachievement in historical perspective. In D. Epstein, J. Elwood, V. Hey and J. Maw (eds) *Failing Boys? Issues in Gender and Achievement.* Buckingham: Open University Press.

Crookes, G. and Schmidt, R. (1991) Motivation: reopening the research agenda. *Language Learning* 41(4): 469–512.

Dörnyei, Z. (1998) *Teaching and Researching Motivation.* Harlow: Longman.

Dörnyei, Z. (1994a) Motivation and motivating in the foreign language classroom. *The Modern Language Journal* 78(3): 273–84.

Dörnyei, Z. (1994b) Understanding L2 motivation: on with the challenge! *The Modern Language Journal* 78(4): 515–23.

Gardner, R. C. (1985) *Social Psychology and Language Learning: the role of attitudes and motivation*. London: Arnold.

Graham, S. and Rees, F. (1995) Gender differences in language learning: the question of control. *Language Learning Journal* 11: 18–9.

Helinke, A. (1993) The development of learning from kindergarten to fifth grade. *Journal of Educational Psychology* 7: 77–86.

Oxford, R. (1994) Where are we regarding language learning motivation? *The Modern Language Journal* 78(4): 512–4.

Oxford, R. and Shearin, J. (1994) Language learning motivation: expanding the theoretical framework. *The Modern Language Journal* 78(1): 12–28.

Pintricht, P. and Schrauben, B. (1992) Students' motivational beliefs and their cognitive engagement in classroom academic tasks. In D. H. Schunk and J. L. Meece (eds) *Student perceptions in the classroom*. Hillsdale, NJ: Erlbaum.

Stables, A. and Wikeley, F. (1999) From bad to worse? Pupils' attitudes to modern foreign languages at ages 14 and 15. *Language Learning Journal* 20: 27–31.

Tashakkori, A. and Teddlie, C (1998) *Mixed Methodology: combining qualitative and quantitative approaches*. Thousand Oaks: Sage.

Wigfield, A., Eccles, J.S. and Rodriguez, D. (1998) The development of children's motivation in school contexts. *Review of Research in Education* 23: 73–118.

Williams, M. and Burden, R.L. (1997) *Psychology for Language Teachers*. Cambridge: Cambridge University Press.

Williams, M., Burden, R.L. and Lanvers, U. (2002) 'French is the language of love and stuff': student perceptions of issues related to motivation in learning a foreign language. *British Educational Research Journal* 4: 28.

Contributors

Richard Badger is a lecturer in TESOL within the School of Education at the University of Leeds. He has published articles on legal language, academic listening, teacher education and approaches to writing. He coordinates the MA TESOL at Leeds and teaches on modules on TESOL methodology and language learning.

Mike Baynham is Professor of TESOL at the University of Leeds. He is the author of *Literacy Practices* (Longman, 1995) and a contributor to numerous recent edited volumes on literacy practices and academic writing.

Alessandro Benati is Principal Lecturer in Applied Linguistics and head of department at the University of Greenwich. He has taught Applied Linguistics and Second Language Acquisition in different universities in the United Kingdom. His current interests are in language teaching, second language acquisition theories, the input processing model and the processing instruction approach. He is author and coauthor of various books and journal articles.

Esther Daborn is a Lecturer in the English as a Foreign Language Unit at the University of Glasgow. Her work and publications are in the area of World English, discourse analysis and the use of corpora for developing academic literacy skills. She has worked on communication skills with Electronic and Electrical Engineering students for a number of years.

Alice Deignan is Senior Lecturer in TESOL at the University of Leeds. She is the author of *Cobuild Guides to English 7: Metaphor* (HarperCollins, 1995) and a contributor to numerous recent edited volumes on metaphor.

Fu-hsing Su is currently teaching at the Department of Foreign Languages, National Chiayi University in Taiwan. He received his PhD from the University of Texas at Austin in 1994 and has since then developed research interests in psycholinguistics and applied linguistics. His recent publications are mainly about phonological development of Taiwanese learners of English. In the future he plans to observe critical issues related to interlanguage phonology and speech perception of English L2 learners.

Sandra Harrison is Head of Communication, Media and Culture at Coventry University, where she teaches in the areas of language and social context, technical and professional writing, and information design. Her recent research and publications focus on computer-mediated communication, including the use of email in the workplace, the application of techniques from the analysis of spoken conversation to the discourse of email discussions, the use of politeness strategies to maintain community in email discussions, the phenomenon of 'flaming', the use of and subversion of repair in email discussions, and the negotiation of email discussion topics through metadiscussion.

Nigel Harwood is a Teaching Fellow in applied linguistics and ELT at the University of Essex. His doctoral thesis is a corpus-based study of how the personal pronouns *I* and *we* are used in academic writing across four disciplines (Business, Economics, Computing, and Physics) by 'experts' writing journal articles and postgraduate students writing dissertations. He has published papers on taking a corpus-based critical pragmatic approach to EAP and on the role of the EAP textbook. His main research interests are in the areas of academic writing, EAP, materials design, and corpus-driven pedagogy.

Li-szu Huang is an associate professor of the Department of English of the Kaohsiung First University of Science and Technology in Taiwan. She received a PhD degree in applied linguistics from the University of Texas at Austin in 2003. In the past years, she has been devoted to the research areas of applied linguistics and psycholinguistics. Recently her studies have focused on second language learners' development of semantic knowledge of English words.

Anne Ife is Principal Lecturer in Spanish and Applied Linguistics in the department of Languages and Intercultural Studies at Anglia Polytechnic University in Cambridge. Her research interests lie mainly in the area of second language acquisition and in the learning and use of languages in the multilingual European context. She has published a number of papers on the learning of Spanish as a foreign language and more recently on aspects of intercultural communication. She has also published Spanish learning materials with the BBC and the Open University.

Hiroe Kobayashi is Professor of English in the Faculty of Integrated Arts and Sciences at Hiroshima University. Her research interests include development of L2 writing and sociopragmatic competence, and cross-cultural study of pragmatics and rhetorical organization. She has published a number of articles in international journals including *Language Learning*, The *Modern Language Journal* and *Journal of Pragmatics* with coauthor Carol Rinnert.

Vally Lytra is a Visiting Research Fellow at the Department of Byzantine & Modern Greek at King's College London. Her research interests are in the area of sociolinguistics, applied linguistics, Greek-Turkish bilingualism and English as a foreign language. She participated in a two-year EU-funded project on second language acquisition and assessment of bilingual primary school pupils in Greece and is currently organising the Greek-Turkish Encounters lecture series in the context of the new University of London BA in Turkish and Modern Greek Studies.

Carol Rinnert is a Professor in the Faculty of International Studies at Hiroshima City University. Most of her recent research and publications, coauthored with Hiroe Kobayashi, have addressed the development of academic literacy among Japanese university EFL students. A second major area of interest they are pursuing concerns the investigation of cross-cultural and interlanguage pragmatics, including comparison of request negotiation and public directives in Japanese and English.

Paula Romero-López is the Language Centre Manager at the University of Greenwich. She is currently co-ordinator of an e-learning project on a Virtual Language Centre, which focuses on the implementation of e-learning, both in the existing language curricula through the Language Portfolios, and for self-access and independent language learning. She also lectures in the MA Management of Language Learning. She has taught Spanish as a foreign Language in the University of Greenwich and in different institutions in the UK, including the Instituto Cervantes, the official institution of Spanish government in London. Her current research interests are in second language acquisition theories, input processing and the processing instruction approach, field where she is at the moment researching for her PhD.

Casmir Rubagumya is Associate Professor in the Department of Foreign Languages and Linguistics, University of Dar es Salaam, Tanzania. He is also Director of Student Services at the same University. His research interests are in the areas of language in education in multilingual societies, language and power, language planning, language and gender, and the preservation of minority languages. He has been a consultant on language in education in Africa for several institutions including the Canadian International Development Centre (IDRC), the Tanzanian Ministry of Education and Culture, and the World Bank.

Mary Scott is a Senior Lecturer in Education and the Founding Director of the Centre for Academic and Professional Literacy Studies at the Institute of Education, University of London. Her main research interests relate to students' academic writing, particularly at the doctoral level, and to the learning and teaching of English in schools and in higher education. She has published a number of papers in these fields.

Geoff Smith is Associate Professor at the English Centre in the University of Hong Kong. He is involved with business communication and English for Science students; editing the *HK Journal of Applied Linguistics*; and running MA courses in sociolinguistics and language contact and change. Research interests include language contact and change, in particular the development and use of Tok Pisin, an English-based pidgin language spoken in Melanesia, on which he did his doctoral research and which is the basis of a recent monograph *Growing Up with Tok Pisin.*

Joan Turner is Senior Lecturer and Head of the Language Studies Centre at Goldsmiths' College, University of London. Her research interests are in the role and conceptualisations of language, as well as language use in academic contexts. She has written a book on study skills, coedited a book on writing in the university, and published a number of articles on cross-cultural pragmatics, conventional metaphor, EAP, and academic literacy.

Goodith White is a Lecturer in TESOL at the University of Leeds. She is the author of *Listening* (Oxford University Press, 1997) which was the winner of the Frank Bell prize in 1999.

Marion Williams is a Reader in Applied Linguistics at the School of Education and Lifelong Learning, University of Exeter. Her research is in the area of psychological aspects of language learning and teaching. She is the coauthor of *Psychology for Language Teachers*, published by CUP, and *Thinking Through the Curriculum*, published by Routledge.